Nancie,

Thank you for
your encouragement.
May you know the
hope to which
He has called
you!

With love,
Kim

REAL STRUGGLES, REAL HOPE

A JOURNEY TO TRUTH, TRUST, AND FREEDOM

KIMBERLY GIBSON JOHNSON

WESTBOW
P R E S S
A DIVISION OF THOMAS NELSON

WestBow Press books may be ordered through booksellers or by contacting:

WestBow Press
A Division of Thomas Nelson
1663 Liberty Drive
Bloomington, IN 47403
www.westbowpress.com
1-(866) 928-1240

Cover painting, Truth, Trust, and Freedom: Margo Owens Boden
Photography of Cover Painting: Allison Dalton

Editorial assistance: Leonard G. Goss, GoodEditors.com

ISBN: 978-1-4497-8982-4 (sc)
ISBN: 978-1-4497-8984-8 (hc)
ISBN: 978-1-4497-8983-1 (e)

Library of Congress Control Number: 2013905824

Printed in the United States of America.

WestBow Press rev. date: 3/28/2013

A Dedication to My Family of Origin

He is the smartest person I have ever known. You know, the kind who doesn't have to try hard? As a small child, he was easy to live with, fun to play with, and would let me be the older sister who wanted to tell others what to do.

As we grew older, my respect for him also grew. He is dedicated, kind, thoughtful, and considerate. When he cares for you, he really pours himself out.

His passions are evident by his choice in books. He used to read everything, and there wasn't anything he didn't know and couldn't talk about. I also love that about him.

If I could point out one area of weakness, I would say he didn't know his limits. In his manner with people, he cared too much, too deeply. He wasn't close enough to himself. He took on burdens he was not meant to carry. When he poured himself out into another, he had no one doing the same for him. Living inside himself, he feared that if someone really knew him, he wouldn't be enough. But he was enough and he is enough. He is a treasure, a child of the Most High who knows his every thought, care, passion, and weakness.

To my precious brother who knows better than me about pain and suffering.

★★★★★★★★★★

She was always a spitfire, a little girl with determination and soul who may not have always listened to and obeyed all my parents' instructions.

I remember thinking she was the cutest baby I had ever seen. As I peered over her crib, I pinched her finger, so tiny and irresistible. As she grew into a firecracker child, I loved her spunk, even if at times I would have preferred more peace in our home.

She was my friend as we grew into young women, and we could be honest with each other. In the dressing room trying on clothes we could laugh until we were in tears and no longer standing.

She is quick with her tongue and can let you know what she thinks whether or not you ask her. She may not think so, but her heart is golden. She desires from the bottom of her heart to love and be loved; wanting love more than life, she is easily hurt. Disappointed repeatedly, she lashes back. A cycle not broken brings despair and loneliness. She is lovely and lovable—unmatched by another.

To my lovely sister who knows suffering and determinedly faces it daily.

★★★★★★★★★★

We anticipated her birth as the most special day in our lives. At fourteen, I was in awe of a baby sister, who was tiny, perfect, and beautiful. I cared for her as if my own child. She was like another family inside a family. When I went to college she was four. I married when she was only ten.

A precious and precocious youngster, she talked for hours on the phone with her friends, doing homework, watching television, and generally tying up the line for hours. Whether in art, dance, or writing, she is steady and determined like no other. She thinks deeply and feels widely. I have the privilege of being on the receiving side of her beautiful character traits.

She moved far away when she graduated from college, which was a good thing to do. I love her for her independent spirit, her perseverance, and her striving for excellence. Most of all, I love her heart. She loves and desires good for those around her, and she wants to relate to them by sharing herself, her life, her passions, and her days.

To my sister, my friend, whose destiny is far greater than she imagines.

★★★★★★★★★★

At a young age, I knew my earthly father found hope in God in the midst of the human struggle. He was my rock, a man of faith and principles. Whatever he did, he did it to the fullest. He valued people and was a friend to all he met.

His life, too short, was a hard one, but he didn't think it was less than it should be. He married his high school sweetheart and worked long and hard to support her and their four children. His love for his family and friends, his church, and his penchant for college sports and family history made his life rich.

I am grateful for his life. I want to be like him. He would probably think this book is too personal to share, and he might have advised me not to do it. Honestly, I have had the same thought many times. Yet because my heavenly Father, evident in my earthly father's life, has given me his hope in my own life struggle, I am indebted to share it with those who walk alongside on this earth.

To my earthly father whose faith is now sight.
What joy it must be in his father's house.

★★★★★★★★★

From as early as I can remember, I thought my mother was the most beautiful woman in the world; no mother compared in talent or looks. I was her first, born six months before her father's death, and I was no substitute for him. There are four of us now, but her first three all arrived within three years, and the last eleven years later. She was the eighth child of ten in her own family and perhaps this accounts for childlike attitude as a parent. She was often more of a child herself than a mother. She liked to tell stories about herself and was spontaneous and outgoing. She loved the limelight, and in that way her personality was so different from my reserve and modest one. I was in awe of her. She was a whirlwind of talk and laughter, certainly the most gregarious person in my world. My serious and sensitive nature was always a puzzle to her. Her natural tendency was not tranquil, and she was not able to offer calmness to her children. But her childlike spontaneity and fun kept things light when life was too difficult. I believe she wanted and needed her children to be her mates in fun—a means to childhood again and to escape adult life.

To my mother, precious and loved child of God

★★★★★★★★★

I owe this book to my Creator God, who allows the struggle in order for me to gain much more than I have lost. My most important relationship in life is with my Father God in heaven, through Jesus Christ my Lord. In the pain, he has shown me hope, and I am forever grateful for the journey and the struggle. It takes me back to the Master every time.

To my Creator God. Hope is his story in my life.

★★★★★★★★

A Note on the Use of Names: After much thought and prayer, I have chosen not to name the persons in my original family. Each has a personal story to share, and it is not for me to tell. I have a special bond with each member, and I want to respect and honor their significant and important journeys. What I have shared are my personal struggles that I could not have told without an intimate relationship to every member of my family. With each vignette, I hope readers will see the hope I have found in Christ through these struggles.

ACKNOWLEDGEMENTS

I am indebted most of all to my husband, Gray, for his love, support, and patience through my journey. He has loved me better than any person could and has given me space when I needed it, but more than that, he has stood with me through it all. He is my soul mate, my best friend, and the most loving husband and father to our children. I am especially grateful to my children, Julie and Alan, who have taught me about love. I could never have dreamed them up. I am grateful to God who has given me much more than I ever imagined.

What can I say to express the appreciation and gratitude I have for my friends? They have prayed and encouraged me on my journey in life, as well as on this special jaunt of writing my story. There is not enough space to name them all. Dr. Rick Petronella counseled me, prayed for me, and showed me that God would heal my heart if I let him. Lynn Adams walked with me, prayed for and with me through difficult times, encouraged me in God's Word, and brought me to Women's Community Bible Study (WCBS). Janie Vianey listened, prayed, and encouraged me on my journey, as well as taught me how to receive friendship and how to be a friend. Kim Faison walked with me and encouraged me to find healing through the written Word. Judy Keappler encouraged me from the beginning and stood with me when I shared my story for the first time. Katie

Hendrickson encouraged me to share my story. Debbie Aslinger listened and fervently prayed. Beppie Lever, Julia Mitchell, Ann Neely, and my Montreat family were advocates before there was a book. Bruce and Dana Witt were wonderful guides and encouragers on this healing and writing journey. Sue Allen and the Northside United Methodist Church Writers' Group were my anchors and support group as I shared my story in front of the first large group. Nancy McGuirk and Women's Community Bible Study, my friends from Table Six at Amazing Collection Bible Study, and my friends who meet at Little River from time to time have been true sisters in Christ in their encouragement, prayers, and support. Team Oatmeal and their wives, my women geek friends from Georgia Tech, and all who came to the Lenten talk were amazing supporters who have encouraged me to heal and to share what God has done. They are faithful and true and I am forever grateful for them, their praying lives, and the wonders of their friendship to me. I thank them from the bottom of my heart.

I want to thank Margo Boden for her remarkable and beautiful painting *Truth, Trust, and Freedom* that is the cover of the book. It is truly a gift of love and demonstrates her heart for the truth in Scripture. I am deeply touched and grateful.

A special word of gratitude goes to Leonard G. Goss, my editor, who took my manuscript and made me think a book was possible. I was awestruck when Len took on my work. I received much more than editing because he is a writer and a theologian. The editing is a huge gift, and so is the assurance that it has passed his muster theologically. Len made the heart message of *Real Struggles, Real Hope* come alive and flow with ease.

CONTENTS

Preface

When you're ready, remember that the Lord is sending
you to release the oppressed and to proclaim the year of
the Lord's favor. That is a great work and a high calling.
Do it the best and truest way you know. Then write in a
book what you see.

The Little Handbook to Perfecting the Art of Christian Writing,
by Leonard G. Goss and Don M. Aycock

I am asking God to allow me to write in this book what I see of
his love, power, and freedom. I want the oppressed to know God's
true heart for his children. Knowing the divine heart, so full of
truth and love, means taking hold of what frees us from darkness
and bondage. I know because I was brokenhearted and imprisoned,
and now I am free.

The Lord's favor found me and I cannot stop talking about it (and
now writing about it). The story he has written on my life is a unique
one of hope and passion, and yet it is not without hardship and pain.
I suppose this is not unlike other children of God when he reveals
himself to them. He summons many of us in the darkest night, in the
middle of our deepest sorrow, because in that way we know who it
is who summons us and who it is calling us by name.

God's story in my life is about real struggle and real hope. The Father does not allow us real hardship without also giving us real hope. We may not always see him working in our lives, or acknowledge his presence with us, but the God of all hope is there with us at all times, even difficult times. It is a matter of God's perspective, not ours. The journey is all-important to get us to the new perspective in Christ because that is how God shapes us to be like him. That is what it means to have eternity in our hearts. And having eternity in our hearts brings light to our darkest moments. We recognize God in those moments, and we know that he does not disappoint us.

I hope to share the truth from God's Word and the freedom that only comes from him, as we take him at his Word. I felt prompted by God to write in a book what I see. Then, as I studied Job, I wondered if there was a connection between the book and Job's response to God: "My ears had heard of you but now my eyes have seen you" (Job 42:5). I want my response to be as Job's, and I have asked God to open my heart and eyes to see him and for him to write this book through me.

INTRODUCTION

I write to readers in pain. To those whose pain is most severe, perhaps from the tragedy of losing a child, or a spouse, or from contracting a terminal illness, I pray God meets you here in these pages and that he will be more present with you than you ever experienced. And I write to those whose suffering has not yet been so pronounced. I invite you to identify with the struggler because your share of pain may come to you when you least expect it. That is almost always the way it happens.

God is holy and intimate, and these are not words we can say about anyone else in the universe. He chooses to come to us as he is in Jesus Christ, and if we believe in him, and in the Holy Spirit residing in us, God dwells within and brings us new and eternal life. Yet at no other time does God seem so intimate and yet holy than in the time of our suffering.

I don't know how we can make it in this world without an Advocate, a Savior, one who loves and cares for us in a deeply personal way. How can we be victorious in pain and suffering without someone leading the way, someone who has known suffering and death like no other? Jesus Christ is alive, ever present in our lives, and if we choose him to be our Savior and Lord he will never leave us or forsake us. Instead, he will give us hope now and through all eternity.

Many of my friends already know about my journey, but not necessarily about all of the striving I chose for too many years. I have only recently been able to put some of my story into words and face the pain. But most importantly, I choose now to live in the victory that Christ has given me through the struggle. With gratitude to the One and Only, I share the suffering in my life because it is in that suffering that he has shown me who he is and what he desires for his children.

WHAT IS REAL HOPE?

The Hope to Which He has Called You

I keep asking that the God of our Lord Jesus Christ, the
glorious Father, may give you the Spirit of wisdom and
revelation, so that you may know him better. I pray also
that the eyes of your heart may be enlightened in order
that you may know the hope to which he has called you,
the riches of his glorious inheritance in the saints, and
his incomparably great power for us who believe. That
power is the same as the mighty strength he exerted when
he raised Christ from the dead and seated him at his
right hand in the heavenly realms, far above all rule and
authority, power and dominion, and every name that is
invoked, not only in the present age but also in the one to
come (Eph. 1:17-21).

A note from *Life Application Bible* reads that *hope* is "the complete
assurance of certain victory through God. This complete certainty
comes to us through the Holy Spirit who is working in us." Our
Father God has called each of us to real hope, which is complete
assurance of certain victory through God. He doesn't leave us alone
in the struggles, nor does he leave us without divine power and riches

that lead to certain victory. We have his hope by the indwelling of the Holy Spirit given to us when we choose to believe in Christ and accept his work on our behalf as our Savior.

Why don't we feel hopeful? Where is this hope when we are down? What gives us this kind of hope in the hopeless situation of a catastrophic diagnosis? In the death of a child or spouse? In the loss of a job or a dream? In the betrayal of a friend? If God has called us to know the hope to which he has called us, why don't we have it? I want to delve into this question by sharing what God has done in my life and how he has revealed himself to me. Given a loving God who gives freely and abundantly, certain victory has come to me through the hope to which the Savior has called me—and the same can be said of any Christian. Receiving what God has already given us as believers is a lifelong practice, and we need to remember daily to be grateful that he is God and there is no other.

Huge blessings come with the struggles of knowing the hope to which the Lord has called us, the riches of his glorious inheritance in the saints, and his incomparably great power for us who believe. In the journey, one of the miracles God gives is the power to believe him and take him at his Word. Not only does he give us hope, but riches and power, too. In fact, God's riches are found in human struggles. His riches are stored in secret places. For me, the process of finding this out meant letting go of barriers I used to protect myself from people and from life. When I allowed God in, he gave me freedom to live in a spacious place. I invite readers to let God move into the places of their lives that are barriers to God's love, and to find freedom in him and in the truth of his Word.

His Incomparably Great Power

How do we come to believe in God? How do we believe what he tells us is true? It is only through the work and revelation of our Lord Jesus Christ that we come to know the Father. He continues inviting us to fellowship with him and to know him better, including in our struggles. But for many of us, we struggle with unbelief until God miraculously shows us his love and redemption. Later we can look back and see God's interventions. We see that with each step we took in our own life struggles, God did not leave us or forsake us—not even when we were clearly outside of his plan for our lives. When things got bad enough in my own life, when I was at the end of my own resources, I admitted my need for God, cried out for the power to believe, and surrendered my life. I found that my desires pale compared to a God who is so much bigger than we know until we let him have our lives. He is the author of new beginnings.

THE PATHS WE TAKE WHEN
WE ARE HOPELESS

The Mind in Battle and the Heart in Hiding

"Hope deferred makes the heart sick" (Prov. 13:12). My heart was sick. Probably in a depression most of my childhood, adolescence, and into adulthood, I found it easier to live without the hope of love than to face that it was not there.

It was either yes or no to my mother. With a yes, I betrayed myself; with a no, I felt selfish I hadn't given her what she wanted. There was no living alongside my mother, in community or family, for living with her demanded total submission. Her willingness to hurt people always made me insecure, but today it was her apathy that gave me the most angst. She asked us to take her to the dining room at the retirement home where my grandmother lived the last few years of her life. My mother always told me that my grandmother, her mother-in-law, was more like a mother to her. She wanted to go there to eat, however, and not to visit my grandmother. That felt really cruel to me because I *did* want to see my grandmother. I didn't want her to know we were there at the retirement home and didn't even stop by to see her. My mother thought all this was silly, making a big deal out of not seeing her.

My mother was either in total control of all she surveyed, or she was ambivalent to what was going on around her. She would determine everything we ate, how long we stayed outside, or when we got haircuts, all the way up until we were in high school. She would often do nothing but sit in front of her mirror for hours on end, but from her children she required part-time jobs—which she demanded for us from people in the community.

For my brother, sisters and me, the positions often came at our expense. There is nothing worse than an employer feeling bullied into giving you something. If they asked for something in return, my mother could turn on them instantly. Relationships with others, whether close or not, were a game to my mother, and games were meant to be won. When she got her way or when she was in control, she had the upper hand. If that didn't work out, she turned on the person, even if it was her own child.

I ached inside and wanted to believe this picture of my mother wasn't true, that I was wrong, and that I could repair my relationship with her. I tried. I thought there must be something wrong with me. Then I thought if I couldn't change her, I could change me. I could change to make her see I was worth loving. All I wanted was to fill the void with being loved, but for me this became a destructive cycle of hope and despair.

I am sure my mother wanted the same thing. She wanted to be loved. To get there, she had chosen her way, the way of devouring, of preying on people, of using them up. I was still choosing my way. I wanted her to love me, and when she didn't, I chose other things rather than avoid the pain of her rejection. The times I didn't feel her rejection were when she got her way. Even then she was not satisfied, but while she continued withholding her affection, at least her contempt was not as noticeable in those moments. She had a good time laughing at and mocking others. This was another good way for her to mask her pain. We were her stepping stones to filling her void.

I thought I was unlovely and unlovable. Why wouldn't I be? My mother had all but rejected me. I had no hope and no future. These were my truths. Since there was no hope, I ran after other things. Sometimes, especially when I was young, I ran straight back to her. And always, without disappointment, she validated my despair, unloveliness, and hopelessness. I kept running. I didn't trust others, and I didn't trust myself. I carried what I learned in my relationship with her to all other relationships, and I thought I needed to change myself.

MANIPULATION AND HURT

Every six weeks my mother took me to get a haircut. I screamed and cried and told her I did *not* want a haircut because I did not need one. The hairdresser cut it really short, almost like a boy. I hated the way I looked, and I cried even more as we drove home. My mother would laugh and say how silly I was to cry. "It looks just fine," she would say. *Fine?* Why would anyone want to look fine? I wanted to be pretty with lots of locks of dark hair.

People would tell me I looked just like my mother. This was a compliment to me because I thought my mother was a beautiful woman. But if she ever heard the comment, she would object. "She doesn't look anything like me. Oh, no. I don't think she looks like me at all. Why would you say that?" I would feel like I was ugly and that my mother didn't want to look like me. The people saying that were just trying to be kind, but my mother shook it off. Clearly I was not good enough for her.

Most of the time my mother laughed at my desire to look pretty.

I long ago stopped asking her how she thought I looked in an outfit. I felt it unbearable to hear what she had to say. But even without asking, she would offer, "That doesn't look good on you." "You are not slim. Your brother and sister are thin, but you are not. You know I'm going to tell you the truth. You are just not slim." "Your hair is just too long. You look so much better with short hair."

There were more hopeful times when my mother gave us mixed messages of affection. While sunbathing in the backyard, she would listen to us talk about our days at school. But if one of us mentioned a difficult interaction with a teacher, or a conflict with another student, she would say, "Why would you care about that? You are too sensitive. My children are all too sensitive. I don't know where that comes from, but it certainly does not come from me." We learned to stay mum about things close and personal. There were times she surprised me. When I became severely ill in college, she made the time to take me to doctor visits and then out for lunch afterwards. It was hard during such times not to feel somewhat special to her. My brother, sisters and I never knew what was coming, and thus we were always on the edge of our seats.

My mother chose center stage over her children, which we didn't consider that odd, most of the time. After all, we thought it was normal for a person who was extroverted to be the life of the party. It was when she ridiculed us or made us feel inferior that we knew something was not right. One example of being upstaged by my mother was when she decided to wear a red dress on my wedding day. It was a traditional wedding ceremony, and I was in a long white satin gown and veil. We had six bridesmaids and six groomsmen in a lovely sanctuary. The bridesmaids were wearing burgundy for the Christmas wedding. My friend and my sister, two of the bridesmaids, had red hair, so I didn't think red was a good color for them. Not only did my mother steal all the attention from me and the rest of the wedding party, she clashed with my color scheme. There was no changing her decision to wear her long, flowing beautiful red dress, and the wedding pictures reflect her exuberance over her choice. I didn't let disappointment ruin my day, but I knew in my heart whose day she wanted it to be.

I had been married for a few years and had just gotten my dream job when my father became sick with prostate cancer. This was before all the medical advances of today, and he lived a total of fourteen months with this tumor. I drove home each Saturday to visit him, and then returned to my husband on Sunday evening. The driving time was six and a half hours each way, and I visited twelve hours. I wouldn't take anything for the time I had with him those last months of his life. Yet in his last weeks of life, she was adamant I had not done enough. If I loved her, I was told, I would leave my husband and quit my job and move home immediately.

When my father died, his portion of the family farm was distributed among me and my siblings. A few years later, my mother came up with an idea to have all of her children give her their portions of the family farm because, after all, she was surely more a part of it than we were. We caved, but again I felt the disappointment of her taking a huge and meaningful thing from us.

When my husband and I were in the early years of rearing our children, my mother orchestrated—without my consent—having an adult sibling come to live with us so that I could find a mental health solution for him. Actually, this had happened with another sibling years earlier when I was single and in graduate school, but I had two children at the impressionable ages of ten and three when she concocted the scheme this time. When I found help for him and had to let him go home, she gave me another ultimatum. Though he lived two hours away from her, she asked him to drive to her house in the middle of the night to turn her heat on (because she was cold and there was sleet falling). He had a terrible accident that night that started a devastating trail of events in his life.

Another thing bringing the illusion to an end that my mother really loved us like a normal mother would was when she asked me to talk to the minister about marrying my brother to a person he had just met in a hospital setting. She felt I should help arrange the marriage and, if I didn't, I was no longer worthy to be her daughter. After many words and my refusal, she had my sister's husband do it. Thankfully, my brother escaped the altar.

One of the most hurtful aspects of the relationship with our mother is her desire to keep her children from each other. If she can stir something up, she will. She says things that blatantly are not true to one or the other of my siblings about what we have supposedly said or done. I have learned over the years to keep to myself, especially regarding my sister closest in age to me. My mother has caused a lot of hurt and destruction in this one relationship. It is a game for her, a way to manipulate and hurt this sister and me.

Alone, Ashamed, and Anorexic

The entire house is quiet and dark, except for one light peeking through from one light bulb hanging freely above the sink in the kitchen. As I enter the front door, the light beckons me in. There I stand and reflect over the evening. The loneliness creeps in, and my mind goes to the dark places. No longer in the light with my friends or coworkers, where I wear an extroverted mask, I face myself. And I am my worst enemy. The thoughts overcome me. I open the drawer where the knives are, and I think about it once more.

Why can't I be the smiling and outgoing person I want to be? Or the happy one who has it all together? I want light and peace instead of the dark thoughts and terrible accusations I make toward myself. I am suffocating in my own dread of who I am. I am unlovely and unlovable. What is so wrong with me that I can't enjoy people or life?

The starvation starts. I cannot and will not eat. After a while, the food I try to eat will not go down. My body revolts and gives me great pain when I put something into it for nourishment. At least that is what I tell myself when the desire for food overwhelms me.

The dining hall is where I meet my friends to catch up on the day. I go through the cafeteria line and head towards our usual table and meeting place. Someone comments, "How can you eat that stuff?" Lime Jell-O, cottage cheese, and Diet Coke made up my diet during college years. Few talk about my thinness, even though it is in stark contrast to how I looked when I started college. I deprive myself; that's what I do.

In my office in graduate school I eat one granola bar, which is all I will have that day, until I get home in the evening, when I will make a salad. My colleagues, older and more experienced than I, give me tips on how to handle teaching my freshmen English and composition class. After they leave, I feel the loneliness I have experienced for years, and also the lack of authenticity I feel in myself because I put on the same mask of happiness and calm. I am lonely, afraid, and sad, and there is no calm in me.

As I reached the end of my last quarter in graduate school for my second masters degree, I approached my professor with a few questions and presented my resolve to finish our last assignment. We did not know at the time that the problem we were trying to solve for the Berkeley-Unix operating system had never been solved. Actually, my project partner and I were really close to finishing the program and solving the problem. My professor urged me to finish the project the next quarter, but I told him I was going home. My father was dying. Until my father was diagnosed with cancer, starving my heart and body was my mode of operation in those days. Until I heard his diagnosis, I fed myself only with education and achievements.

ALWAYS RUNNING

I was always running from things. If it wasn't one thing chasing me, it was another. I would climb to one peak and then another; the achievements were always higher and more difficult. The issues with my family continued escalating and I could not get away from them. They wanted me at the center of whatever drama was playing out, and if I refused to get in the middle of it they would accuse me of disloyalty and threaten to disown me. My depression (undiagnosed at the time) never let up. Around me was always a black cloud of doubt, darkness, and despair.

Standing still never seemed like an option. Wouldn't the black hole envelop me if I stopped running? If I stopped running, would I not have to face the issues so confusing me—depression, anger, fear, and loneliness? Problems loomed in every direction.

Now I did not realize it at the time, but I was running from myself. It is a strange thing that we think we can outrun something inside of us. I felt completely deficient, knew it in my bones, but I didn't want anybody else knowing it. The thing to do was keep running. No one could understand my trauma. Who else knew from an early age that she could not trust her own mother? What oldest child would allow the terrible things done to her siblings at the hand of their mother? What daughter would abandon her family just to save her own life?

Running became a way of life. When I was with my mother

and siblings I made the best of it I could. When I left them, it was in terrible emotional pain and upheaval, and it took days to recover from the chaos and deceit. Then I would run back to my own home to the other side of life, which had me running in another direction entirely. I began wondering when I could stop and get off of the treadmill of life. I needed a break, but if I took one, what would I do with myself? I kept wondering and slowly began waking up.

I did not want to struggle with the things I knew were at the end of the running. I was already in severe circumstances, and I believed it would be worse if I stopped. In effect, I was trying to escape. Where was hope? At the time I desired hope, but I didn't think it was possible as there were too many big forces taking it from me as they did in the past. My mother was still taking things from my siblings and me. The stability we were making for ourselves in our young adult lives didn't last long because my mother would make bold moves putting disorder and fear back into our lives, like when she moved a sibling into another's apartment. In addition, I believe I always suffered from depression, but because I would not share my deepest needs or concerns with anyone, no one knew. And that was just the way I wanted it.

SHAME AND SELF-RELIANCE

The ideas of shame and self-reliance seem paradoxical. There were times I felt ashamed of myself, but I still relied on myself to get things right, to do the right thing in the right way. Why would a guilt-ridden person continue relying on herself totally? We don't always know we are acting out of shame. Our past actions or the consequences of our past actions keep us in shame. The actions or consequences of someone else in our lives can also give us reason to be ashamed. No matter where it comes from, or why, shame reaps bad outcomes.

I have had several seasons of shame, all of which brought on bad results. I was anorexic in college. Anorexia nervosa is a serious eating disorder where I had an excessive fear of gaining weight. Consequently, my eating behavior meant I was malnourished and underweight. This abnormal condition can lead to many negative effects, some of them severe and lifelong. In my case, the anorexia led to a disease I will have for the rest of my life. Because this was before the media ran stories of the disease, no one at my college, or anywhere else that I knew of, had ever heard of "anorexia nervosa," the behavior of controlling the intake of food. My shame was that I did not feel loved or valued by anyone, least of all myself, which I did not want to admit. I felt invisible, so I tried to make myself invisible. Growing up, I lived in a very controlled environment, which appeared orderly on the outside to those looking in, but it was chaotic on the inside. I went to other people's homes, but they did not come to mine. Desiring something other than what I had, I lived in books, music, and my schoolwork. I was not comfortable with myself or with others, and this made me feel like a fake person, an invisible soul. I was very deep and intense about what I saw and felt, and I wanted very much to get out of myself and into whatever was out there. Anorexia was an outlet to have a little part of me in control of some aspect of my life, even one I found shameful.

Another season of shame was the first few years of my marriage. I didn't feel worthy of the marriage or of the family into which I had married. I was invisible again, not one to love or cherish. I developed unhealthy relationships in order to cope with my shame. I was drawn to people who were manipulative and who could make me feel like I was needed and loved. It was where I felt comfortable because it was familiar, and this is a dangerous and slippery slope. I knew the game I was playing, but it was bigger than me, and I was acting out of shame and self-reliance.

Eventually my shame led me to cry out to God, who is always available and waiting for us to admit we are in need. Shame can make us run to others and other things when we don't feel worthy of God or his mercy. And the truth is that we aren't worthy of God or his mercy. But even so, God wants to have a relationship with us. He gives us mercy through the gift of his Son, Jesus, not something anyone of us deserves or can earn.

My guilt has kept me from God at other times in my life. Again, self-reliance makes me think I can earn what I desire. I want to get it right in order to come before God with my plea, but I misperceive what it is God offers and have failed to grasp the width and depth and height of divine love. God got it right for all time when he sent his Son to enter the human condition to live and die and rise again. Because God sacrificed his only Son for us, we don't have to get it right. We have to receive it—his Son, his sacrifice, his gift to us. We choose to receive what he offers us freely and without cost. There is no cost because God paid the price, and in gratitude we accept the gift of righteousness. And when we do receive it, God sees us as he sees Jesus, making salvation a gift we cannot earn. It can only be free.

Striving, trying to earn and achieve love, life, and things are some of the ways I have had to learn that God is there. Without him, none of the achievements or striving means a thing. The big hole in my life will remain the big hole in my life if it is not filled up with God himself, and that I cannot achieve or earn or buy. God is God, and there is no other. Our shame and our guilt are walls that keep us from the miracle of God's great love. We cannot do for ourselves what God has done for us. As simple as it sounds, our pride keeps our hearts and ears from knowing and hearing his heart for us, but it does not have to keep us from the Father himself.

I WAS READY TO LIVE

"The medicine isn't working!" I call out to my brother to take me to the emergency room. Though the smoldering heat seems to have triggered my over hydrating, I am weak from dehydration, and my body continues depleting itself of fluids. My teeth chatter, even though it is hotter outside than I have ever felt it in my life. As the rest of my body shivers uncontrollably, I realize I need help immediately. Grateful that my brother is visiting me in my apartment where I live while in graduate school, I know he has already called my mother to ask what he should do.

My mother was not as concerned as me about getting to the hospital, but I urged my brother to take me. In defense of her, there had been many times since I was diagnosed with diabetes insipidus that doctors would see a college-age girl looking thin and visibly weary and respond immediately that I was on drugs. It was the age and culture in which we lived in the mid to late 1970s. But I was afraid of drugs and alcohol, and the DI was enough for me to handle during those years. My brother hurried to help me to the car, and with a blanket wrapped tightly around me, we drove in silence to the closest hospital.

As they placed me on the stretcher in the emergency room, a physician approached and asked me to tell him what was going on. Fearing he might laugh at my response, because I thought I was dying, I told him I was losing consciousness. Surprised that he stayed by me, I kept answering his questions as long as I could.

When I awakened, the attending physician stood by my bed and looked at me with surprise. "Do you know what a miracle you are? You almost slipped into a coma and died last night. We need to do some tests to see what the problem is." This was not a surprise to me after the many years of baffling doctors with my disease, so I responded with a nod.

The next few days continued the nightmare beginning with the heat and dehydration. The one sure test that patients conclusively have diabetes insipidus, not to be confused with diabetes mellitus, is to deprive them of fluids and observe them continue to deplete the necessary fluids in the body by urination. They gradually lose a significant amount of water weight over the course of a few hours. As they deprived me of water or anything else to drink, I became weaker as my weight dropped from the depletion of fluids in my body. My mouth was parched, my body was weak, and my natural and strong desire to drink water was overwhelming. After a designated period of time, and before the test caused serious complications from fluid deprivation, the physicians gave me an anti-diuretic hormone, a drug that acts the same as the hormone the body lacks in the disease of diabetes insipidus. Even though we already knew I had the disease, the test reconfirmed it. I was just ecstatic to get a drink of water; nothing ever tasted so good.

The next day, a neurosurgeon entered the room and stood by my bed. Alone in the hospital room and only twenty-three years of age, I hear him say, "You have a brain tumor. We need to do some extensive tests: a spinal tap, a CAT scan, and a pneumoencephalagram." I nodded. Although strange to hear news of this sort, I knew my ordeal was serious. Still, I hadn't quite gotten its significance until now. The first two tests proved positive for a brain tumor, which they thought was the reason for the diabetes insipidus, only discovered with these procedures and previously not detected. Prior to this my doctors thought my disease was idiopathic, meaning they would possibly never know why it occurred.

The hospital sent me home to my apartment until I was strong enough to do the main test—the pneumoencephalagram. I could not finish the summer session in my graduate work, so I had plenty of time

er immense aogrly
efhead

on my hands. I cried out to God, "I want to live." I don't know that I ever felt like I was dying after the night of the emergency room, but I did think that I wanted to make my life count now. It was almost as if when I awakened after the slow loss of consciousness, I knew I had a fresh start, even with the doctor's prognosis. The day finally came for the big one, the pneumoencephalagram test. During the procedure I was fully awake. One instrument blew air up my spine into my brain and it hurt worse than anything I have ever experienced. Four nurses held different parts of my body so that they could do the procedure and see all areas of my brain. As I threw up and complained of an immense headache, they assured me I was doing well.

As I left the operating room, the physician called out to me, "No sign of a tumor. You are going to be okay." Amazing words for this twenty-three year old. I was ready to live. Was I really?

No Escaping the Heart

There is no escaping the heart. God made us to be relational, and that is why we want to love and be loved. When my husband and I were dating, it was a blissful time. When he showed up in our singles' Sunday school class, I saw a cordial but stiff person introduce himself to our class members, one by one. The thought that ran through my head at that moment was that he looked like the man I would marry. "*Whoa.* Did I really have that thought?" I said to myself. Not long after, he asked me out. From the first date in February to our engagement in September to the wedding in December, we had known each other less than a year. But we each knew we had found the one. It was his sense of humor that drew me in. We laughed and talked through many meals and outings. My heart opened to him. Not only did he have similar interests and goals, we had similar spiritual beliefs. I believed that I had found the man God planned for me.

After the wedding and honeymoon, he moved into my apartment. This was an awakening when all my husband's stuff took up a lot of space, and when he moved my things around at whim (*Ah, the joining of two as one*). We enjoyed our time together there, even though it was short lived. Before long, we headed off for him to go to graduate school. He remembers one night especially fondly in our small apartment when he woke up as I was looking out the window and telling him to come see the snow. There was no snow, just a streetlamp casting a white glow on everything. My only explanation was that when you live in the south and dream of snow, at times you can see mirages.

The years in graduate school flew by. We made the most of the time with friends and family. Most of all, we really got to know each other, warts and all.

THE HEART AWAKENED

Sometimes it takes something drastic for the heart that has been hidden in a life to wake up. It was 5:30 AM on a Friday morning as my father and I drove forty-five miles to a regional hospital for his biopsy. We talked about college basketball team forecasts, the weather, and what the weekend held. But looming in our minds was the life-changing procedure he was about to undergo. While my father had been in pain for months, and the doctors had done a lot of tests, none showed anything to alarm them. This test, however, was the one we didn't want. I asked him if he was scared, and he told me he was—just a little. But he said he had had a good life and that if it was his time to go, then so be it. I didn't like this attitude at all, but I didn't let on to him. Mentally he was stoic, but his body was strained in pain as he sat in the passenger seat while I stared ahead at the road.

When we drove home later in the day he was weary but pensive. Finally, he spoke. "You need to go ahead and have children; it's time. What are you waiting for?" he asked, not in a pushy way but in a way that was wise and fatherly. I did not say it at the time, but we were trying to get pregnant. It was a poignant moment, one I will never forget. I asked if there were things he wanted to do in the next few months after he got well. Still encouraged that this was just a test, I wanted to talk about future trips and fun times together.

Still the stoic, he reminded me his life was good but that he felt that the prognosis was probably not going to be. The day was dark and gloomy, not just because fall was turning into winter, but because one life was going to be changed forever. My father, diagnosed with prostate cancer at age fifty-five, lived only another fourteen months. In his attitude and faith he was a wonder to many, most especially me.

God works in mysterious ways. I spent many seasons of life absorbed in head knowledge. Hiding from my heart was a way of life for me. Working on my second masters' degree when my father was diagnosed with prostate cancer, I was in a state of disbelief and horror that life might have to go on without him. Nothing would have taken me from my academic pursuits except my father's state of health. I definitely would not have let it go for my own personal heart issues. For him, however, I would let it go to take the time he had left to better know him and love him. My heart ached at the prospect of losing him. He was my anchor, the rock in the family. At some level, I knew his death would be the beginning of many other devastating losses.

My heart was vulnerable to life; I did not trust anyone or anything, and I was not accustomed to being in plain view of others. But now my suffering was not private, and neither was my father's. He especially did not like this state of affairs. Where was God going with this? I felt betrayed and abandoned one more time with my life and the people I loved the most. I cried out to God to heal my father, to make him well, and to allow us more time together. But God did not heal him, at least not on this side of life. And while we did have time, it was not enough, although it was more than we expected. My father gave each day all he had, smiling in public and grimacing in private with the pain. He treated his in-home caregivers with the utmost respect and love. Every weekend I had with him was a gift, and I think it was to him, too.

MARRIAGE, MORE STRIVING, AND MOTIVATION FOR CHANGE

They say a marriage is only as healthy as the least healthy partner, and the statement rings true. There are always difficulties when two people become one in marriage. My husband will have many crowns in heaven for living with me. I am married to my soul mate. They also say that it is more common to end up in the marriage counselor's office if the husband and wife come from families where they are both oldest children. As two oldest children married to one another, we are grateful to our Christian counselor, who has been crucial. And we know that God has a sense of humor in putting us together.

We are both pleasers and achievers. I am less critical when speaking than is my husband, but I am probably more so in my mind. We have a difference in temperament. He personally likes critique and says what comes to mind. I have a difficult time with criticism because I tend to draw the wrong conclusions and feel very hurt by critical words. When he is trying to communicate, my tendencies make it harder to work through the issue at hand.

So it goes in marriage when we bring things to the partnership from our previous experiences. My past trust issues, such as my mother saying hurtful things, color how I perceive my husband's words, to whatever extent they are spoken in love or good intentions. I hear them as from someone who hurt me in the past. Baffled, he tries harder to communicate. The communication gets worse because I'm unwilling to go there. It is often true that we cannot face what hurts us. It blocks us from having the good in the present.

I work hard to please everyone, and so does he. I bring my lack of love and trust and intimacy issues, and he brings similar ones. Striving in our marriage became routine, in large part because of me. I regret this because it takes joy from life, our lives individually and as a couple.

Was I uncomfortable enough to want something different? Was I ready for change yet?

THE REAL STRUGGLE—WHERE THERE'S HOPE

What I lacked in relationship, I attempted with my mind. My husband and I both have an intellectual side and a relational one. I favored staying in the books or music, and I preferred being on the surface with my peers. But I knew that there was a void. I was afraid somehow of really getting in there where it might hurt, and this was true even with my husband. It doesn't have to be one or the other, the mind or the heart. Necessarily it is both, for God desires wholeness for his children. No battle is necessary between the mind and the heart, but in my case, my mind never ceased in striving to fill the void in my heart. My heart, screaming for attention, knew the emptiness.

Will She Know that I Love Her?

Round and round I walk the neighborhood with the same question constantly nagging: "Will she know that I love her?" It is part prayer and part bashing my head up against a wall. In the midst of working day in and day out, being a mother to a toddler, and being a wife, I am tired and frustrated with myself for not being satisfied with all I have. I have a great husband, a precious daughter, and work that is challenging and fulfilling. But the question will not go away.

The reason it will not go away is that it still exists. I don't know my own mother's love. I continue praying that my own beautiful and wonderful child will know that I love her.

Life is difficult when you work all day, try to keep a house, continue being a partner in marriage and a mother to a child. The list is as long as the day. Even weekends don't come when your work is in a startup. The pressures mount for me to be a good wife, mother, and employee, and I want to please everyone. Yet I please no one, least of all myself, on this merry-go-round of life.

I look at my life and what my child might see when she looks at my life. I'm doing a list of things, not very well in my opinion, although no one else has told me that, only to start doing the list all over again. Does my daughter see the unsatisfied and striving mother I think I am? Does it look to her like I love other things more than I love her? Or more than I love myself? Could she see that? I definitely didn't want to model self-loathing, or one who goes through life without joy in the moment. My search continues for a better mother for my daughter.

One day it happens. I am praying as I walk around the curve in the road. It is almost as if I hear God saying to me, "She knows you love her." I'm overwhelmed with the intimacy of the moment. God heard my prayer. I didn't consciously ask, but he answered me. And he says she knows. I pick up a stone to remind me I don't have to continue fretting over this question anymore.

Freed. The desire of my heart is met by God. "What else might he be doing?" My heart craves more.

Facing the Pain and Looking to God

Living in the pain of my mother's apathy toward my siblings and me, and her willingness to hurt us, propelled me to search for hope. I looked for it in many wrong places. After years of running, despairing, and settling, I finally had the courage to call the pain what it was. It was the pain of my mother's lack of love for me, my sisters, and my brother. I don't like admitting that, not for her, and not for me or my siblings. Facing the sadness, cruelty, harm, injustice, and longsuffering of my siblings and me has given me courage. Persevering through the painful relationship with my mother is day after day, but naming the truth has allowed me to see other things, too. I have grown in ways I did not think possible because I faced down the enemy—the pain in the situation and the shame and sorrow of the ongoing struggle.

When God didn't fix my mother—or fix me so I could fix her—I thought he let us all down. I am still disappointed in several outcomes of the pain and ongoing struggle. Facing the death of many dreams and fears has made me stronger. I don't have to carry the dreams or fears either anymore, or pick them up to bring them to fruition. If I look to the bottom of the blackness and face it head on, God does not leave me there. Somehow facing the worst gives me hope. Knowing the truth frees me. The gravity of the evil is lighter because I know the hope. Hope overcomes. Light stands in and over the dark night, and it wins now and tomorrow.

Acknowledging that pain exists and facing it head on gives us courage. When we know we cannot fix it or control it, we know that courage is necessary. It is living in the struggle that grows us in ways we never imagined. The pain changes us; we hope for the better. If we deny its existence, we still have the struggle or the pain. When we take paths to avoid the suffering, we create more pain. Facing the truth, however painful, gives us courage and hope. In Romans 5:1-5, the apostle Paul says that our suffering gives us perseverance that builds character in us, and from it, we have hope. He wrote, "Therefore, since we have been justified through faith, we have peace with God through our Lord Jesus Christ, through whom we have gained access by faith into this grace in which we now stand. And we boast in the hope of the glory of God. Not only so, but we also glory in our sufferings, because we know that suffering produces perseverance; perseverance, character; and character, hope. And hope does not put us to shame, because God's love has been poured out into our hearts through the Holy Spirit, who has been given to us" (NIV). Paul is referring to the hope that will not disappoint. Why not live in that kind of hope while we are in pain?

In my heartsickness, depression, loneliness, fear, and sadness, I knew that going to God was the only way. I have seen the ravages of heartache and despair in my two siblings; I am disappointed beyond words for their ongoing pain. But there is hope in the present and hope for the future, including the hope of glory. I am not running to fix my family of origin anymore. I am no longer expecting God to fix those things I want him to fix. My new pleasure is just expecting God. I can see his hand because I am looking for him. He is so much bigger than I give him credit for. I know he has carried me more of the years than not, and I believe he is carrying my siblings, too.

Some days I focus on the disappointments in all of it. Why doesn't it get better? Why don't they get better? I realize these are not the right questions. I can reach for God's hand and hang on, or I can stay inside myself and feel worse. These are my feelings, but they are not truth. Then I go back where God got my attention twenty years ago. It is his truth that matters. He is where I place my hope. I do not hope in my feelings because feelings are not a good measure of truth. There is always disappointment, but at the end of the disappointment is God. I may be hurt and have questions, but God is God and there is no other. This is a working faith, not a blind one. I take one step at a time. And at the end of the day, there is faith.

No longer Bound to Hopelessness but Beckoned to Something Else

Awakened by severe pain wrapped around my chest, I tried to move. My mind started to race. Should I get help? Only my daughter was at home with me. My husband was on the Appalachian Trail with my son. It was not even 2:30 in the morning. Could I get to the phone and dial 911? Should I wake my daughter and drive to the emergency room? Could I manage the pain until I got help? I held my chest and tried to sit up, but I was scared to move. I decided to lie back down on my pillow. The pain kept coming, but I didn't think it was my heart. It would be okay to stay in the bed until I knew what to do. I couldn't control it, but then I couldn't ignore it. I had been learning to lean into what I didn't want to face. I had to succumb to the pain wrapped around my chest.

Usually I would not advocate this attitude for physical pain. When awakened for any physical pain whatsoever, especially if it might be heart-related, I would not advise laying back down. But in this case God gave me an epiphany through my physical pain. By awakening me in the wee hours of the morning, God awakened me to a truth he has been teaching me: When I realized I couldn't control the pain wrapped around my body, I let go; when I let go, I became less agitated. I began praying as I lay there. My body was motionless as if the quietness in my mind was taking over. It seemed like I was there for maybe an hour, quietly accepting in the pain. When I awoke I was no longer in the awful pain anymore but instead I was beckoned to something else.

God was there all along, when the pain woke me up, when it kept coming, when I went back to sleep, and when I awoke to its shadow. I didn't know his presence because I was focused on the pain, and even more on how to stop it. He was there, but I couldn't see him when all I saw was pain. At any time we choose, God will give us a new view. I woke up remembering the severe pain, and wondering if it would come back when I got up, but I also woke up remembering even more that God was there in the night in my struggle. He gave me his presence and his rest.

This experience taught me much about my emotional pain in real-life struggles. It taught me that I need to face head-on the pain that God wants me to let him handle. I knew if I gave the pain to the Lord that I would have a new view. Sometimes when the road changes, we are forced to see a different panorama, a dramatically new scene we have not seen before. We have a new lens and a new perspective. But at other times, we have to let God have our view so he can change it. I believe it is like this with hope—hope in God. He can give us a new view, his lens on the pain, the struggle, and the suffering. I still remembered the pain; the shadow was still there. But now God was beckoning me to his view, to a new hope.

I believe this was a discovery of utmost significance in my life. I learned I could run from the struggle where I was running from myself. I could endure the suffering and be stoic. I could be a victim where I would establish blame or shame. Or I could lean into it and learn through expectation. In this way, I had hope in God. I had a choice in the matter. I could choose God. I could also choose to let God change me instead of the struggle or the pain.

My new discovery was that instead of being a woman holding onto herself, I could have eternal hope in God. My mother's deficiencies and my own deficiencies were pitted against God's wholeness and hope. I had to let it be. I could not stop it, or change it, or control it. I let the pain of it be; I stepped into it. And all of a sudden, I awakened to its shadow. No longer was I in the awful struggle anymore, but I was beckoned to something else.

LIVING IN HOPE AND BELIEVING GOD

Real struggles give birth to real hope. Hope is not in pain or the absence of pain, but real hope comes from going through the struggle and finding hope outside of ourselves in God. When we do, we see he was waiting there all along for us to let go in him. When I learned I could not change the course, I leaned into it and let go. Against all hope, I hoped.

God gives us hope when we accept Jesus as our Savior, and we receive the gift of the Holy Spirit, who dwells in us in the struggle or pain. Because of the grace of God, Jesus' suffering and shameful death on the cross are things we will never have to endure. Jesus endured sorrow and pain like no other, and he did it for us, to die for the sins that should have been on our heads. The Holy Spirit gives us the power to believe in the atoning death of Christ and to have the hope we could not muster on our own.

I always wanted my mother's words to mean something. I always wanted to count on them. I wanted to be certain who she was in my life, and what she meant for me. I believe those are desires God places in us as we look to him. To live in hope means that we know in whom we have the hope. The book of Hebrews says that "God did this so that, by two unchangeable things in which it is impossible for God to lie, we who have fled to take hold of the hope offered to us may be greatly encouraged. We have this hope as an anchor for the soul, firm and secure" (6:18-19). We can believe what he has to say because God is the unchangeable one for whom it is impossible to lie. His character remains the same yesterday, today, and forever. What he promises and when he promises is certain. He is who he says he is, and he does what he says he will do. Living in hope is living in the certain knowledge that God is the God of all hope.

Living in Hope and Enduring the Struggle

Hebrews 12: 1 says, "Therefore, since we are surrounded by such a great cloud of witnesses, let us throw off everything that hinders and the sin that so easily entangles, and let us run with perseverance the race marked out for us."

The concept of faith is defined in the book of Hebrews as, "now faith is being sure of what we hope for and certain of what we do not see." (Heb. 11:1) The eleventh chapter of Hebrews goes on to describe the heroes of the faith and how God planned his best for them and that they believed him by faith. The twelfth chapter begins with a charge to throw off all that hinders us from the race of faith so we can run with perseverance the race marked out for us. Isn't this how we come to hope? God beckons us with his best for us, and we choose to believe him. When something bad occurs, however, how many of us wonder if God really has his best in mind for us? How many ask, "What did I do wrong for this suffering to occur? How long does God intend for me to struggle like this?"

To live in hope, the writer of Hebrews says we have to throw off everything that hinders us, including the doubt and the sin. He points us to Jesus, the author and perfecter of our faith. This is what he writes: "Let us fix our eyes on Jesus, the author and perfecter of our faith, who for the joy set before him endured the cross, scorning its shame, and sat down at the right hand of the throne of God"

(Heb. 12:2). Jesus, who loved us so much, died a shameful death and endured unequalled pain while dying on the cross. The writer anticipates that in our own lives we will have questions and we will have pain. And when the race gets tough and things get us down, he reminds us to fix our eyes on the One who has lived through the pain, abandonment, and the sacrifice. Moreover, Jesus sits at the right hand of the throne of God and intervenes for us in our faith walk, in our journey of hope that gets derailed by daily living in pain or suffering.

Does the sin that so easily entangles us include our doubt to believe God? Or our desire to fix the very struggle God uses to bring us into a deeper faith? I believe it does because in my own life God has used my deepest pain and sorrow to strengthen the hope I have in him and his Word. He has used my unbelief to show me that his character is true and his promises are sure. To bring me back into his arms, God used the tangled web of lies and deceit that I formerly believed. Eventually I had to throw the lies down so I could hang on to the truth he taught me to run the race he had in front of me.

It is like climbing a mountain with a backpack. If the pack is too heavy, you can feel yourself toppling backwards. Or, when you take a couple of steps forward you feel yourself step back to get grounded in order to take another pace ahead. It's like that when we are trying to hold on to things we are not made to carry. God tells us in so many different ways that we are not burden-bearing animals. He wants us to let go and let him carry the burdens. To run the race God has in store for us in this life, we cannot lug around all the baggage we try to carry. In my case, the baggage was the lies and deceit I believed. And I discovered I could not carry the burdens of the ones I loved in order to feel like I was caring for them so they would love me in return.

God didn't create us with the strength necessary to carry loads of this nature. He gave us the free will to choose him, trust him, and decide to let him be our guide and strength. If I tried holding on to the past and walking in the present, I couldn't. I just didn't have the wherewithal or the strength. But if I let go, that was another story. He would carry it for me. It is like that with the sin that so easily entangles in that we have to throw it off. Then we can endure the race set before us and have the capacity for it when we place our hope in God for the race and whatever it entails, whether joy, pain, blessing, or struggle.

When we live in hope and walk in faith, we look to the One who gave us hope to endure the struggle. He died for us and showed us that we are the joy set before him. In addition, the Lord gives us the capacity to remember this truth. If we ask him to change our view when it gets warped, he gives us the real thing and gladly gives us a fresh pair of eyes and a new heart to keep our attention on Jesus, the author and perfecter of our faith and our real hope.

God's Work of Redemption and Necessary Suffering for Believers

Through Christ's death and resurrection, God's work makes us into people who please him and who do work that pleases him. The apostle Paul says in Philippians 3:10, "I want to know Christ and the power of his resurrection and the fellowship of sharing in his sufferings, becoming like him in his death." It was in sharing what he knew of Jesus that brought the apostle joy. Even if sharing Jesus' message meant great suffering, Paul was committed to tell others about the life-changing story of the One who was sent by God to save humankind. Paul identified with Christ's suffering and knew the joy coupled with it because he knew Christ's message of hope was getting through to the people.

Hebrews 12:2 says, "Let us fix our eyes on Jesus, the author and perfecter of our faith, who for the joy set before him endured the cross, scorning its shame, and sat down at the right hand of the throne of God." Jesus' shameful death on the cross was for the joy set before him—meaning all humankind. He endured the shame and the cross for us, because it gave him great joy in setting us free from the consequences of sin. Paul knew this joy, too; he preached it and wrote it so others would know the gospel of Jesus Christ.

In Romans 5:1-5, Paul tells the Christians in Rome that suffering will occur and that it will grow their perseverance and their character. Here is what the text says:

> Therefore, since we have been justified through faith, we have peace with God through our Lord Jesus Christ, through whom we have gained access by faith into this grace in which we now stand. And we rejoice in the hope of the glory of God. Not only so, but we also rejoice in our sufferings, because we know that suffering produces perseverance; perseverance, character; and character, hope. And hope does not disappoint us, because God has poured out his love into our hearts by the Holy Spirit, whom he has given us.

With suffering, perseverance, and character, Christians have hope in Christ, whose hope does not disappoint. Again, Paul knew suffering was inevitable, but he also knew it was a necessary part of growth for believers, just as it had been for him.

Joy is incomplete without suffering; hope cannot be found without the necessary struggles. Without things that are uncomfortable we would have no growth in things good, better, or best. To have God's best requires that we know he allows hardship to show us who he is. It is for his name's sake that he shows us who he is, and it is through the difficulties in life that we see him for who he is. It is for our joy that God gave us Jesus, his only Son, because we are his joy. Hope found in Jesus comes through God, who knows what it takes for us to have hope. When we struggle and suffer we die to ourselves, and this is how it should be. Death to self is life in God, because the death of Christ is life to us.

From the time I was in high school and attending a Bible study grounded in the Word of God, I fell in love with a verse in Paul's letter to the Philippians: "I want to know Christ and the power of his resurrection and the fellowship of sharing in his sufferings, becoming like him in his death" (3:10). I believe that God stirs his Word in us even when we don't know exactly what it means yet. This verse, which was a puzzle to me at the same time it was a comfort, was truth. The Holy Spirit gave me this thought to hold onto through the years. We even had a melody that we put to this verse, and I sang it all the time—"I want to know you, Jesus." In coming to know Jesus personally, I would know his power and his suffering, and even his death. These were new ideas, and I craved to understand what they meant in my life. God is Truth and he is faithful.

A few years later, when I was in graduate school and had a very close brush with death, the verses from Romans 5:1-5 became very important to me. This time I was looking for hope. Paul wrote about rejoicing in the hope of the glory of God. God gave me hope in this Scripture because I knew he was shaping me through this near-death experience. "Hope does not disappoint us, because God has poured out his love into our hearts by the Holy Spirit, whom he has given us." I knew this was true, and I held on to it when, in addition to life and death matters, turbulent academic times made daily living unbearable. My major professor did not get tenure, and I failed my comprehensive exams, which was a huge blow to my ego and my plans for finishing the master's degree. God remained by my side, and I knew I needed to place my hope in him rather than in a course of study or an academic program. I was getting to know him in the trenches, as it were. It was in the valley of lost hope and confidence that I sought his Word, and this made me want to dig deeper. He was my only hope.

At the same time, my family was going through strife of its own. My mother sent my younger sister to live with me, not because I needed someone with me, but because it would be better for everyone (meaning my mother) if my sister lived with me. My sister was depressed and needed to be away from home. I'm sure my mother convinced her she was helping me by moving in. It was very hard to be in my own struggles and at the same time watch my sister's chronic emotional pain. Her depression was depressing me, even though I was probably in a state of depression on my own—but I just did not want to admit it. Again, God wanted me to lean on him for hope rather than my mother, sister, or anyone else in my family. Anyway, they were too involved in their own problems and actually wanted me to solve theirs for them. At the bottom myself, I was miserably disappointed in them. Now I was isolated, alone, and helpless. I had nowhere to turn for emotional encouragement or even financial help; I was on my own.

God had me just where he wanted me. Out of his mercy, I started a Bible study and invited others to join me. Why not put hope in the works from the origin of despair? It was in this Bible study group I led that I met my now husband. He was the one who encouraged me to finish the master's degree and to continue along the academic path I had started when the trauma began.

It is wonderful to look back at Scripture, such as Philippians 3:10 and Romans 5:1-5, that God has made alive in my life. Scripture has been pivotal in my getting to know God and giving me insight into who he is and what he wants me to know about him. His redemptive work was yet underway while I was still struggling to know God and believe him. I didn't trust anyone most of the time. When I did, I was often bitterly disappointed. It made for a difficult life, relating to friends, family, and especially a new husband. God used my unbelief and my struggles with relationships in huge ways in my life's redemption story. I stayed in the valley until I wanted no more of it, and he came to my rescue. Sweetly and slowly, he allowed me to see myself for what I was and had become, a self-reliant, angry, depressed, and lonely woman who would not and could not trust anyone. I wanted out of this miserable life where there was no achievement, no dream, nobody to help. I was full of self-pity, shameful pride, and unforgiveness. I thought it was hopeless.

God uses low points and self-despair in our lives. He allows us to get to the end of ourselves. Not only were there terrible circumstances in my life, but I was reacting to them in ways that were not working. It is true that times were rough and a lot of it was not my fault. But I was also not the person I wanted to be, and the more I worked on it, the less I became, or so I thought. I could not grow myself into the person I wanted to be. I could not achieve the things I wanted and be fulfilled. I could not please everyone else and be true to who I was. In order to live, and I mean really live, I had to die to a lot of things I had chosen to live by, including pleasing, achieving, desiring to be known, and being appreciated by the ones closest to me. God really had his work cut out for him with me. I was a lifelong struggler with things God did not necessarily have in mind for me, and yet he had not given up on me. He was still waiting patiently for me to let go and let him have me to bring real hope out of real struggles. I finally cried out to God for help.

Isaiah 43:10 says,

> "You are my witnesses," declares the Lord, "and my
> servant whom I have chosen, so that you may know and
> believe me and understand that I am he. Before me no god
> was formed, nor will there be one after me.

I suspect we all struggle with believing God at times. That is just our human nature. But God gives us the ability to believe him with the indwelling of his Holy Spirit after we have come to faith through Jesus Christ. It is through our struggles that he reveals himself to us and shows us who he is. There will be mountains to climb, deserts to wander, and mighty seas to traverse. Each is a reminder that God is with us. If it were not so, we would not be able to handle our lives here on earth. He desires that we take him at his Word by making one step of faith at a time.

God gives us the strength to handle the most difficult situations. In the New Testament, Ephesians 1:19-20 refers to the glorious Father's "incomparably great power for us who believe. That power is like the working of his mighty strength, which he exerted in Christ when he raised him from the dead and seated him at his right hand in the heavenly realms." The strength comes to those who believe as God goes with us through the hardest things. In Isaiah 43:1-7, the Bible says that God will be with us when we pass through rivers and walk through fire:

> But now, this is what the Lord says—he who created you,
> O Jacob, he who formed you, O Israel: "Fear not, for I
> have redeemed you; I have summoned you by name; you
> are mine. When you pass through the waters, I will be
> with you; and when you pass through the rivers, they will
> not sweep over you. When you walk through the fire, you
> will not be burned; the flames will not set you ablaze. For

> I am the Lord, your God, the Holy One of Israel, your Savior; I give Egypt for your ransom, Cush and Seba in your stead. Since you are precious and honored in my sight, and because I love you, I will give men in exchange for you, and people in exchange for your life. Do not be afraid, for I am with you; I will bring your children from the east and gather you from the west. I will say to the north, 'Give them up!' and to the south, 'Do not hold them back.' Bring my sons from afar and my daughters from the ends of the earth—everyone who is called by my name, whom I created for my glory, whom I formed and made. "

The Isaiah text does not say the Lord will be with us *if* we pass through waters and walk through the fires, but *when* we pass through the waters and walk through the fire. God knows you by name, and He has created you for Himself.

God knows his children well and he allows them to wander. There are times when our direction in life is not clear, but the Lord is present to guide and protect. In Psalm 121, the psalmist declares the Lord's help, protection, and goodness:

> I lift up my eyes to the hills—where does my help come from? My help comes from the Lord, the Maker of heaven and earth. He will not let your foot slip—he who watches over you will not slumber; indeed, he who watches over Israel will neither slumber nor sleep. The Lord watches over you—the Lord is your shade at your right hand; the sun will not harm you by day, nor the moon by night. The Lord will keep you from all harm—he will watch over your life; the Lord will watch over your coming and going both now and forevermore.

The Maker of heaven and earth is with us in everything. He

is there is to protect, to guide, and to give strength. He is also there to comfort and to give us perseverance. He modeled these things in Christ Jesus. God's compassion and love for his children, a mystery manifested in the life, death, and resurrection of his Son, is also revealed in Scripture. The prophet Isaiah says, "'Though the mountains be shaken and the hills be removed, yet my unfailing love for you will not be shaken nor my covenant of peace be removed,' says the Lord, who has compassion on you" (Isa. 54:10).

In order to believe God, we have to have an encounter with him on a personal level, and then stay in communication with him through prayer and the reading of his Word, the Bible. He provides us with insight, understanding, and truth as we learn and grow closer to him. God says that his Word was from the beginning: "In the beginning was the Word, and the Word was with God, and the Word was God. He was with God in the beginning" (John 1:1-2).

Believing God is a continuing process of stepping into faith on a daily basis. It is a journey in which God calls us to trust him by knowing and believing who he says he is in his revealed Word. Believing in God is a decision, and believing God daily is a choice. When I look back at my life, I believed in God from a very early age. In fact, the age of nine I decided to follow Jesus as I listened to a Billy Graham message during an evangelistic crusade—but I think I believed in God even way before that. Believing God daily, however, has for me been a longer road. I have been a hard case, a stubborn, striving, ashamed, and relentlessly untrusting girl-then-woman. But God has been good to me, never condemning, ever merciful, and always pulling me back.

When we believe God, we have the ability to know hope. As the Holy Spirit gives us the capacity, we can see things from a hopeful stance. But we may also choose to fear, worry, despair, and rely on

39

our own striving or strength instead of turning to God for all the strength we will ever need. Trusting in ourselves is misplaced and precarious, as is placing our hope in another person or in a particular outcome.

God gives us free will to make life choices to believe or not. He tells us, "This day I call heaven and earth as witnesses against you that I have set before you life and death, blessings and curses. Now choose life, so that you and your children may live" (Deut. 30:19). With each thought and action we either determine to follow and believe the Lord, or we choose not to follow or believe him. Sometimes we are not aware that we have chosen death over life because we are so deceived by what we think is true. But God will reveal his truth to us as we offer our deepest longings and our deepest fears to him.

What is the Writing on Your Wall?

In the gospel of John we read, "You will know the truth, and the truth will set you free." (John 8:32). Let me share a personal encounter. In my mind's eye, a little girl crouches in a dark and cluttered hallway closet. Mountains of stuff fill this tiny room where she remains hidden from everyone and everything. Besides the stuff of anger and doubt in this small space, the walls have writing on them that names the fears, insecurities, and reasons for shielding herself from the unfamiliar and the unknown. Many times, the little girl tries to exit her safe place. With a mask of self-prescribed extroversion, she determinedly leaves the four walls of her secret domain to be good at things and people—a good student, wife, even a mother. Hesitantly, she tells herself that hope and joy are within reach. But after a short stay away from the security of the hallway closet, the little girl goes back inside and continues hiding from life.

I was that young girl, and I built the four walls around myself to be a shield from discomfort and pain. There were times I tried leaving that closet to achieve something that I thought would bring freedom. It never did. Trapped inside the tiny space I had no idea what I was supposed to be or who I was supposed to please. I shut others out and basically shut myself down. It was miserable, yet familiar, comfortable, yet lonely. I was saddened that life was not more than this. I did not want to live this way any longer, so I cried out to God—who had been with me all along. He knew my pain and insecurities, my anger and fear. Bigger than any wall of self-protection I built, God would bring down these walls if I let him. My crying out was the first step.

We think the familiar and the known are somehow the safest and surest places, and this sounds logical. But it is not true. I developed thought patterns that became familiar and true to me, but ultimately they were lies that kept me hiding from life and the living. Somehow I thought that God was there, but he had failed me by not protecting me or my family members from harm.

When I cried out to God, he drew me close. While giving me an undeniable thirst for the Bible, the Lord taught me how to know him, pray, and accept him at his Word, concepts that were new to me. Each lie I believed created thought patterns and actions that crippled me, a part of the support of the huge wall I built, and I had to face each one. God began taking pieces of the wall down just far enough for me to see his hand and just small enough for me to handle. I have seen how intimately he chose the timing with his gentle compassion throughout this difficult, yet soul-freeing process in my life. It became a habit after a while to take each thought through the paradigm of his Truth. God drew me to him, heard my heart's cry, and then grew belief in me. In the wall's place was the truth and armor of the Almighty.

God has "set my feet in a spacious place" (Ps. 31:8). He has given me courage to live without walls around my heart. The little girl who refrained from living because it was too painful has found comfort in the Savior's arms. As a now grown woman, I'm compelled to tell the Lord's story in my life, for he is like no other.

What is the writing on your wall? Whatever keeps you from living in freedom are strongholds that only God can bring down. He is our strong tower, our deliverer, our fortress, and a very present savior. Let him have your deepest hurting places; he will fill them with his truth and love. "Then you will know the truth, and the truth will set you free"(John 8:32).

Remember, we are children of the King. If we are brokenhearted, he can bind us up. If we are in the dark, he can make us see. If we are imprisoned and in chains, he can set us free. The prophet Isaiah knew this when he wrote, "The Spirit of the Sovereign Lord is on me, because the Lord has anointed me to preach good news to the poor. He has sent me to bind up the brokenhearted, to proclaim freedom for the captives and release from darkness for the prisoners, to proclaim the year of the Lord's favor and the day of vengeance of our God, to comfort all who mourn" (Isa. 61:1-2).

I know God can bind us up, make us see, and set us free. I know because he did it for me, a little girl crouching in a dark and cluttered hallway closet.

Belief—the Truth versus the Lies

Becoming acquainted for the first time with who God says he is in Scripture was the most transforming experience of my life. Every day I craved God's Word and literally prayed the Psalms. From them, I found a kindred spirit in the heart of David and the other psalmists who poured out their raw emotions and feelings and didn't hold back their cries of sorrow and pain. For the first time I began facing my struggles instead of hiding and running from them. David's descriptions of and awe for God stirred something in me. They made me want to believe the God in the Psalms. When I prayed the songs in God's Word, my heart started to change.

These were tumultuous times as the emotional and mental upheaval of my family hit me full blast. Their demands were too much for me, and I was not spiritually or emotionally strong enough for their onslaught. I became severely depressed and faced my despair head on. King David's cries from a downcast soul became my threnody. I believed God heard my cries, and deep down I thought he would change my circumstances. Belief was a crucial first step.

God is so much greater than my imagination. He began a work in me that is his story in my life. I thirsted for God's Word and I could not get enough of the Bible. I did Bible study in groups and found more to do on my own. I was living and breathing what God fed me, and it became my daily bread. The Father broke the barriers in me that kept me from him by transforming my mind and exploding my life struggles. God's truth landed on the soft soil in my heart. My own devices led me to depression, but God's hand was there and I reached out for it. Scripture tells us that "the Lord himself goes before you and will be with you; he will never leave you nor forsake you. Do not be afraid; do not be discouraged" (Deut. 31:8). Beginning with this truth, God revealed himself to me, and through his Word he showed me the lies I believed, one by one. The story of God in my life begins with God, who gave me the thirst for divine truth. He then showed me how to discern the lies I had believed from the truth in his Word about who he is and why he cares.

Believing that God loves me was a major breakthrough. God himself never changes, but he surely transforms us if we are willing. God taught me about my unbelief and showed me how to pray for him to heal my unbelief. And he taught me about his love. 1 John 4:16 says, "And so we know and rely on the love God has for us." While on a visit home, I awakened to the truth that God loved me. Reading the Bible in my childhood bedroom, I was astounded and amazed that God's Word was alive and being spoken right to me, a parched and starving soul. As fresh as the new day, the words resounded and became true to my believing heart. God's sweetness was so real, allowing me to know his love back in the home of my youth where I struggled to know love. For the first time, I knew that the little girl in me and the grown woman with children of her own was loved by her Father God. In these few precious moments I was set free to be who the Creator made me to be.

After this major transformation, God revealed many other areas of my unbelief. Along with showing me who he is, the Lord also gave me an incredible desire to know him and believe him. He was not only giving me new truths to live by, but new hope and new thinking. A new heart full of hope replaced the old one full of fear and despair, and I rejoiced with new expectations and dreams.

Then He Breaks the Barriers in our Heart so We can Know Him

I began living with a new foundation of Christ Jesus at the center of my life, with God's Word and Holy Spirit as my guide for daily living. The old partition came crumbling down, while new ones of truth, trust, and freedom began forming in its place.

With new focus and a transformed perspective, I began walking by faith, one step at a time. God guided me to new places, unfamiliar ones not necessarily in my plan or on my path. Replacing old habits and patterns of thinking with God's Word produced new challenges.

If I didn't believe the lie anymore, then what did I believe? It was like God was challenging me to let him test my barriers. I wanted them to come down because I now knew that what God provided in its place would not only be better, but it would be God's best for me. He was peeling away layers of old thinking and patterns of unbelief and replacing them with his heavenly perspective.

Each time I would come to a new and yet unfamiliar place, God provided his presence and his Word to guide me. Yet trusting God felt like a mountain to climb. I knew he could give me the faith of a mountain if I asked, but I kept trying to climb the mountain on my own. As I prayed and cried out with my petitions and pleadings, and though I received no answer that gave me an understanding of my circumstances, God told me in not so many words, "You are the mountain; get out of my way." Well, I finally got it.

God not only gives us faith, but he grows the faith. He increased my faith by revealing that I was the mountain, and that I needed to move aside for him to be in charge. As we get to know God, he softens our hearts and restores our souls. We are the clay in the potter's hands. When he tells us to move, we move. I got out of his way that day. He left me in the same circumstances, but I felt his presence and his moving in my heart in a new way. He was changing me.

I thought I was letting go of barriers when God told me I *was* the barrier, standing in the way of what he was trying to do. How little we really know about how God sees us. God says, "'For my thoughts are not your thoughts, neither are your ways my ways,' declares the Lord. 'As the heavens are higher than the earth, so are my ways higher than your ways and my thoughts than your thoughts'" (Isa. 55:8-9).

God was moving me to new places in my heart that had never been touched before. He was also moving my husband and me from a home we had been in as a family for over sixteen years. It began with restlessness over our children. As I look back, this restlessness could only come from God's heart. We had tried for many years to buy a new home, only to grow weary of the search. God wanted us to trust him in this search for where he wanted us to live. He impressed upon us Proverbs 3:5-6, which reads, "Trust in the Lord with all your heart and lean not on your own understanding; in all your ways acknowledge him, and he will make your paths straight." We did not need to understand, but to lean on the Lord. I was learning to trust God in ways I had never imagined. Now I was trusting God for my marriage, where we lived, where we worked, and where our children went to school. As I looked the metro area over for schools, the words in Psalm 31:8 came to mind: "You have not handed me over to the enemy but have set my feet in a spacious place." My heart opened more to the mercy and grace of our great God as I observed his hand guiding us to the spacious place where he wanted our children to go to school.

Daily Walk in Expectation of God, His Presence and His Hand

When we know God's truth, we are able to test what we perceive and discern its veracity. There is a yardstick, a standard to measure what is right and what is wrong. With the Holy Spirit as our guide, we also have the ability to view things and experiences through the lens of Christ and the Word of God. When relying on God and the Bible's teaching becomes a daily practice, we receive a deeper and wider capacity for discernment and wisdom from the Ultimate Reality himself. When we know and live the truth of God, he sets us free to live the way he planned all along.

We bought a new home that God knew about long before we

did. He knew what we needed as a family, and he brought us to a spacious place. He had given us hearts to trust and follow as he led us to the perfect location and home. It was our Jordan River that we crossed on dry land (Josh. 4). At first, we had no idea where we were going; we only knew God had closed all the other doors and led us to this one. We felt like we were blind and had no ability to determine right from left, but we knew we could follow the path he determined in advance for us to take. Through the years we had our dream house list, so we knew what we wanted in a house. We also knew what types of schools would be good for our children, and what neighborhoods they served. But we could not bring all this together on our own. With a short window in which to make a decision and move from one house to another, we were in a bind. School had already ended for the year, and it would start again in just a few weeks. Where were we to move? Our daughter was going to summer camp and would not return home until school started. Would she return to a new home?

In one short weekend, God led us across the Jordan's dry riverbed. My husband and I visited the high school one more time on Friday before making our final decision on the school district. When we did, God made it really clear we were in the right place. The real estate agent scheduled a viewing of a few houses for Saturday. As we walked in the first one, we knew that we were in the right home. Being cautious and deliberate about big decisions, we had never experienced anything like this; we actually made an offer later in the day. We were crossing the Jordan and we knew the magnitude of God's faithfulness. God's spacious place for us was tangible and real. He set our feet in a spacious place to live in his truth and freedom by trusting him in all things, including our lives and the lives of our children.

The power and grace of God became even more real to us through this experience, and it awakened in me a new desire. I wanted to shout it to the mountaintops. I was new to this kind of thing.

TRUTH

Jesus answered, "I am the way and the truth and the life. No one comes to the Father except through me" (John 14:6).

This day I call heaven and earth as witnesses against you that I have set before you life and death, blessings and curses. Now choose life, so that you and your children may live and that you may love the Lord your God, listen to his voice, and hold fast to him. For the Lord is your life, and he will give you many years in the land he swore to give to your fathers, Abraham, Isaac and Jacob (Deut. 30:19-20).

Seven Truths about God's Character

God gives us the Holy Spirit to illuminate his Word in our lives. As we grow in Christ, we can discern biblical truth from the lies the world wants us to believe. The key component to knowing God and his character is time spent reading Scripture. The following material explores seven truths about God. Knowing God is much more than having head knowledge, however. It is about knowing him in the heart.

God's character remains the same yesterday, today, and forever, and his promises are certain. He reveals his character and attributes through the actions recorded in the Bible, both the Old and New

Testaments. Two things are sure about the God who made us: He loves us and he never leaves us. The rest of this book illustrates God's love and mercy for us, and his unfailing ways of staying with us and near us.

God is Intentional

Often our culture depicts God as a capricious being, one who does things without forethought or plan, some good and others chaotic and unexplainable. God is always deliberate, never chaotic in nature, and he never acts in unplanned ways. His actions may be inexplicable to us; after all, he is God and his ways are not our ways. The prophet Isaiah has it this way: "'For my thoughts are not your thoughts, neither are your ways my ways,' declares the Lord. 'As the heavens are higher than the earth, so are my ways higher than your ways and my thoughts than your thoughts'" (Isa. 55:8-9). God is intentional; he creates, loves, disciplines, judges, reigns, redeems, and is everlasting. None of these things show that God is either malevolent or impulsive in nature. Far from it. He is holy, set apart, other than humanity and higher than humanity. And yet God created men and women in his own image and made himself accessible to us through his Son, Christ Jesus.

If we examine Scripture we find examples all throughout that God is involved with his people and acts in ways that are consistent with his character. He does what he claims he will do, for that is his nature and his design. There are many accounts in the Bible that show how intentional God is. These include stories of God's people from the beginning including creation, his covenant with Israel, his deliverance of them from slavery to the Promised Land, life with the kings and his direction to them from the prophets. The accounts also include God's plan in the birth, life, death, and resurrection of the

Messiah, Jesus, and his intentions for the salvation and re
of all creation. Moreover, God clearly shows his purp
children's everyday lives as well.

> The Lord had said to Abram, "Leave your country, your
> people and your father's household and go to the land I
> will show you. I will make you into a great nation and I
> will bless you; I will make your name great, and you will
> be a blessing. I will bless those who bless you, and whoever
> curses you I will curse; and all peoples on earth will be
> blessed through you" (Gen. 12:1-3).

God established a covenant with Abram and told him to leave his
home and go to another land. He promised to make a great nation
from Abram's family and descendants. God chose Abram to be father
of the nation and he told Abram the plan and showed how his family
would be blessed:

> The Lord said, "I have indeed seen the misery of my people
> in Egypt. I have heard them crying out because of their
> slave drivers, and I am concerned about their suffering.
> So I have come down to rescue them from the hand of
> the Egyptians and to bring them up out of that land into
> a good and spacious land, a land flowing with milk and
> honey—the home of the Canaanites, Hittites, Amorites,
> Perizzites, Hivites and Jebusites" (Exod. 3:7-8).

God cared about the abuse of the Jews. He wanted them out of
Egypt and into a new place, one that would be good, spacious, and
bountiful. He intended good for them and provided them with a
new home.

> The Lord said to Samuel, "How long will you mourn for
> Saul, since I have rejected him as king over Israel? Fill
> your horn with oil and be on your way; I am sending you

to Jesse of Bethlehem. I have chosen one of his sons to be king." …But the Lord said to Samuel, "Do not consider his appearance or his height, for I have rejected him. The Lord does not look at the things man looks at. Man looks at the outward appearance, but the Lord looks at the heart (1 Sam.16:1, 7).

God chooses the prophet Samuel to anoint the new king, whom God has chosen from one of the sons of Jesse. As they go through the process of selection, God eliminates each son until Jesse tells Samuel that one more son is tending the sheep. When David arrives, God tells Samuel to anoint him king. God was clearly intentional in choosing Samuel to anoint David king. His plan involved incalculable details, which God executed down to the smallest elements, including all the years David served as a shepherd preparing to become king.

For the eyes of the Lord range throughout the earth to strengthen those whose hearts are fully committed to him (2 Chron. 16:9).

God says that people look at the outward appearance, but he looks at the heart. He intends good for his people, and he desires to find and strengthen hearts of those who love him.

"For I know the plans I have for you," declares the Lord, "plans to prosper you and not to harm you, plans to give you hope and a future. Then you will call upon me and come and pray to me, and I will listen to you. You will seek me and find me when you seek me with all your heart. I will be found by you," declares the Lord, "and will bring you back from captivity. I will gather you from all the nations and places where I have banished you," declares the Lord, "and I will bring you back to the place from which I carried you into exile" (Jer. 29:11-14).

God plans our todays and our tomorrows, and they are plans for good, not harm. He is intentional in his love and his plans to give us a hope and a future.

> He went to Nazareth, where he had been brought up, and on the Sabbath day he went into the synagogue, as was his custom. He stood up to read, and the scroll of the prophet Isaiah was handed to him. Unrolling it, he found the place where it is written: "The Spirit of the Lord is on me, because he has anointed me to proclaim good news to the poor. He has sent me to proclaim freedom for the prisoners and recovery of sight for the blind, to set the oppressed free, to proclaim the year of the Lord's favor." Then he rolled up the scroll, gave it back to the attendant and sat down. The eyes of everyone in the synagogue were fastened on him. He began by saying to them, "Today this scripture is fulfilled in your hearing" (Luke 4:16-21).

God decided to live with us by entering the human situation in the form of God the Son (in Jesus). We see in the verses above that Jesus went to the synagogue to fulfill the Scripture in Isaiah where God revealed to his people the year of the Lord's favor. God is intentional and consistent in his character, word, and actions.

> For God so loved the world that he gave his one and only Son, that whoever believes in him shall not perish but have eternal life (John 3:16).

The righteous and holy nature of God demands justice and all sins must be recompensed. And that is why God took on human form and came to live among us in the person of Jesus. Jesus came to die for all sinners. The Father determined how, when, and where his Son would die so that all of his children could have eternal life.

The meaning of this is plain: God has intentions for us; he knows our days. His greatest plan for us is to know him personally and spend our lives in relationship with him. He gave salvation to us in the ultimate gift of his Son, Jesus. God's intention is for us to worship him and live out his plan and purpose for our lives. We may choose to enter a relationship with him or not, but either way he loves us. The Creator loves all of his children. If we look at our lives in retrospect and in the now, we can see God's hand. The presence of God has always been with us, and we will never be without it.

MY STORY OF UNBELIEF TO BELIEF AND GOD'S INTENTIONAL CHARACTER

God does not do anything by accident. Neither does he tell us anything in his Word that is untrue. The fact that he is intentional gives me great assurance and hope. As Isaiah 55:8 tells us, "'My thoughts are not your thoughts, neither are your ways my ways,' declares the Lord." Yet God does make us aware of who he is and what he wants for us. For example, we are told in Psalm 25:14 that "the Lord confides in those who fear him; he makes his covenant known to them." God is intentional, and he wants us to know him and his promises. My story is one of unbelief to belief, stretching from my head to my heart. I know now that God intended it down to the very last detail.

So far as I can recall I have believed in Jesus from the time I can remember believing in anything. Yet I still remember watching a Billy Graham crusade on television when I was nine. After hearing the message, I knelt by my bed and asked Jesus to come into my life. God gave me a wonderful church family who nurtured me and assured me of Jesus' presence and love.

Many years ago, I was in a deep depression and knew I needed help. I was seeing a Christian counselor, and many of my friends were praying for me. My family was struggling with mental health issues, and I had gotten in the midst of some pretty tough things with them, which I couldn't control. Several friends recommended I go to a particular Bible study, but I was just too depressed to do anything social. In the gap, God gave me an incredible craving for his Word.

My husband is a very supportive spouse. At the time my children were in elementary and middle school and I didn't want the problems of the family where I grew up affecting them. But they were. What was I to do? I wasn't going to get better until something changed, or rather until I changed. I had worked on the other things changing because changing me seemed out of the question.

One morning at the Christian counselor's office, I took the Bible study workbook that I had just begun on my own. He said something that lingered with me: "I want you to throw it in the trash if you do it with your head. But if you do it with your heart, it will really help." At any other time I would have gotten angry, pouted like I was being reprimanded, and at the same time been really down on myself for being criticized. Yet the Holy Spirit was already at work in me receiving these words and convicting me in a way that God uses best.

The Bible study encouraged me to look at the strongholds in my life and my patterns of unbelief. It also suggested I look back at my family of origin and review how I interacted with them and what I felt about myself regarding to them. During my time doing the study, I visited my mother several states away. My husband encouraged me to go and to "bring back the little girl inside of me." Petrified, because I knew something big was happening, I took the trip to the home of my youth. God was changing me. As I learned (in my heart, not just my head) through God's Word, I struggled with believing that God loved me. As a child, I knew in my head that God loved that my church and my family loved me, but I had closed my heart when hurtful things happened. And of course in those years hurtful things happened all the time. Criticism and judgment were a matter of course.

On the second day of my visit, an amazing thing happened in the home where I grew up. As I was doing the Bible study in my former bedroom, I read the following Scripture from First John 4:16: "And so we know and rely on the love God has for us. God is love. Whoever lives in love lives in God, and God in him." I reread this verse and substituted "I" for "we" and "me" for "us": "And so I know and rely on the love God has for me." I knew it was true. God loved me. I had written "Father, heal my unbelief" in the margin of the study the day before. Now he had healed my unbelief. I believed in my heart that I was beloved of God, and I could now accept the fact that I was a child of the King. He loved me, not because I was related to someone, married to someone, a friend of someone, or in the church with everybody. He loved me for just being me. My heart was at rest while his blessing permeated my whole consciousness. What joy overtook me! Psalm 16:11 wasn't kidding: "You have made known to me the path of life; you will fill me with joy in your presence, with eternal pleasures at your right hand." This was absolutely true and absolutely God's intention for me!

We do not always know exactly what God's intentions are for us, but we know they are for our good—as the apostle Paul tells us in Romans 8:28: "And we know that in all things God works for the good of those who love him, who have been called according to his purpose." God is intentional in his ways and in his Word; his actions are just and merciful and intended for our best. There is nothing in God's economy that is wasted. Everything accrues for the benefit of the children of God. From the most tragic things to the most benign things, God molds affairs to his purposes and our good. We are often awestruck at how small details work into the greater plan of God's will, and yet from our mountains of disaster his hand forms miracles.

GOD IN MY LIFE? HOW DO I KNOW? WHAT DOES IT LOOK LIKE?

It is through a relationship with Jesus Christ that we know God is who he says he is. It is in a personal relationship with the Son of God that the Father reveals himself to us. Does life sometimes seem haphazard or capricious? Why do so many feel life is accidental or not intended for them? In order to search for God's intentions we have already reviewed several events and characters in the Bible. Here are two more. In Abraham's old age, God made a covenant with him to make a great nation through him. Sarah was nearly ninety when she gave birth to Isaac, Abraham and Sarah's son. When Moses was a baby, he was placed in the Nile River to escape being killed by the Egyptians; however, later his own mother reared him in Pharaoh's household. God greatly used Moses to free the Israelites from Egypt's enslavement. There are many more examples inside the Bible and out, including ones in your life and mine. What we consider haphazard or capricious God may have intended for our good.

God Favors His Children

> Therefore, say to the Israelites: "I am the Lord, and I will bring you out from under the yoke of the Egyptians. I will free you from being slaves to them, and I will redeem you with an outstretched arm and with mighty acts of judgment. I will take you as my own people, and I will be your God. Then you will know that I am the Lord

your God, who brought you out from under the yoke of the Egyptians. And I will bring you to the land I swore with uplifted hand to give to Abraham, to Isaac and to Jacob. I will give it to you as a possession. I am the Lord" (Exod. 6:6–8).

God desires good things for his children because he favors them. Even when we act like we are not favored by God, or when we disobey God, he remains steadfast in his love and compassion and desire to draw us back. After God delivered the Israelites from the oppression of the Egyptians, he reminded them of his love and his commandments.

I will look on you with favor and make you fruitful and increase your numbers, and I will keep my covenant with you. You will still be eating last year's harvest when you will have to move it out to make room for the new. I will put my dwelling place among you, and I will not abhor you. I will walk among you and be your God, and you will be my people. I am the Lord your God, who brought you out of Egypt so that you would no longer be slaves to the Egyptians; I broke the bars of your yoke and enabled you to walk with heads held high (Lev. 26:9–13).

When Jesus was born in Bethlehem, the angels appeared and sang, "Glory to God in the highest heaven, and on earth peace to those on whom his favor rests" (Luke 2:14). God brought a Savior, his Son, into the world because he favored people so much. He freed them from failing to live by his commandments by giving them the gift of a Savior. In Paul's second letter to the Corinthians, he urges his readers to believe that the day of salvation has come to them.

As God's co-workers we urge you not to receive God's grace in vain. For he says, "In the time of my favor I heard you, and in the day of salvation I helped you." I tell you, now is the time of God's favor, now is the day of salvation (2 Cor. 6:1–2).

God favors me. I cannot get my thoughts around this, and the Lord doesn't expect me to "get it." What he does expect is that I accept it and let it grow within me. One way that I let it grow is by remembering how he has shown me his favor throughout my life. This seems like a good place to be today. He no longer wants me to dread what might happen because now I realize he is always with me. Though I may not have recognized him, he has always been in my life. My habit of dreading the uncertainties of life has lessened over the years because I have learned through Scripture that we can renew our minds through Christ. God's Word applied to life makes all the difference in the world in how we see things. When in doubt, I go back to what is true. God's Word is true. If what I am thinking is true, then it will line up with the teachings in God's Word. If not, then it is a lie. Just because we feel or think something does not mean it is true. When I am worrying or dreading life, I am usually thinking a lie. God's truth in his Word says that he favors us, and God's actions throughout all human history show us this is true.

> The secret things belong to the Lord our God, but the things revealed belong to us and to our children forever, that we may follow all the words of this law (Deut. 29:29).

It is fair to say that we don't understand God. And this is no wonder because he is greater than we can ever imagine. We cannot comprehend his ways or his thoughts, and yet we know he relates to us and wants to be in relationship with us. Even this notion is incomprehensible. When God reveals his mind, we have part in a special relationship in which the God of the universe, who is holy and perfect beyond measure, shows us himself, and makes himself available in an intimate, knowing way. He makes himself known to us, and his presence becomes our hope and our desire.

We do not have a hold on the secret things of God, but according to Deuteronomy 29:29, the things that God shows us belong to us forever. We can pass them on to our children, and they can pass them on to their own children. In fact, this is what God wants us to do. When we sit and when we rise we are to tell them our stories of his faithfulness so that we can trust and obey God in our lives and so that others may know that the God of Abraham, Isaac, and Jacob is the Lord God of the universe. What a compelling thing to know what the Redeemer has revealed to us. We are special in that the Lord has given us a very intimate, personal, unique relationship with him, the one supreme God.

I want to know the things God has revealed to me. I hunger for them. The real thing is to know him, for he is the mystery revealed. And when we do, we have the best promise, the most awesome secret to the heart, and the life-giving news that only the gospel bears.

> I want to know Christ—yes, to know the power of his resurrection and participation in his sufferings, becoming like him in his death (Phil. 3:10).

He offers true satisfaction because he favors us and gives us a thirst quenching invitation to come to the waters.

> Come, all you who are thirsty, come to the waters; and you who have no money, come, buy, and eat! Come, buy wine and milk without money and without cost. Why spend money on what is not bread, and your labor on what does not satisfy? Listen, listen to me, and eat what is good, and your soul will delight in the richest of fare. Give ear and come to me; hear me, that your soul may live. I will make an everlasting covenant with you, my faithful love promised to David. (Isa. 55:1-3).

God's invitation is to all people in all lands of all races and creeds. He bids us to come to him to find nourishment that will satisfy, food that is the richest of fare. And when we come, we must accept and receive what God has to offer. The Lord of the universe is offering us food that will satisfy and sustain us. The same Creator who knit us together and knows us inside and out offers us the life only he can give. If we accept the invitation and receive God on his terms, we enter into an everlasting covenant with him, a promise that entitles us to have nourishment that delights our souls.

There are times we have a thirst so strong that whatever we drink is not enough. We keep drinking water until we can't hold anymore. When I am like this it reminds me that our physical and spiritual bodies inhabit the same place, that perhaps my desire for more water is a metaphor to get me to God right now. In Isaiah, the prophet reminds the Israelites that God is available, that he is better than all else, and that he will satisfy as no other. Come, all you who are thirsty, come to the waters! Do we look to God our Father as the One who satisfies, who provides what is good (and free no less), and who will give us the richest of fare so that our souls delight?

All other places we choose to go for peace and joy and rest will not satisfy. We can go to our jobs, live out our parents' dreams for us, live vicariously through our children, or just fill our lives with busyness and things. God alone can quench our souls' thirst. When we come to God, who is the wellspring of life, he is there waiting for us and ready to satisfy whatever the thirst may be. *But we have to come.* When we come to the giver of life, he gives and we receive. What do we receive? We receive what can satisfy us, which is God himself. In addition, we receive strength for the race today, compassion to serve his people in his world, words to proclaim the Lord's faithful love, and rest for the body and the soul.

Food and water only last our bodies for a period of time before we need more, but God is always available and with us as we receive him daily. Again, we have to come. He is with us, but we have to acknowledge him and give our days to him so we are ready for his Word, guidance, and teaching to fill us up. And as he gives, we want more and more because he is the only One who can satisfy. When I want more, God is there for me, and my soul is quenched with his living water. And when I can hold no more, he holds it for me for the next time as I continue growing in faith and obedience. Let us come, souls thirsty, expecting to be filled. God wants to continue blessing us so the world will know him, the One and Only.

In the fifty-fifth chapter of Isaiah we are reminded of God's covenant with David. "Give ear and come to me; hear me, that your soul may live. I will make an everlasting covenant with you, my faithful love promised to David. (Isa. 55:3). This became the covenant to all who call on the name of Jesus Christ through the lineage of David. All nations or peoples of the earth will look to Christians to find Christ because God's children are endowed with splendor. He has given us much for which the world will desire and wish to receive also. He also reminds us to seek him and call on him and receive his mercy instead of forsaking him (Isa. 55:6-7).

Finally, God reminds us that his thoughts are not our thoughts, and our ways are not his ways (Isa. 55:8-9). He is a holy God, separated from sinners, yet he desires communion with us. Isaiah chapter fifty-five closes with: "My word that goes out from my mouth: It will not return to me empty, but will accomplish what I desire and achieve the purpose for which I sent it. You will go out in joy and be led forth in peace; the mountains and hills will burst into song before you, and all the trees of the field will clap their hands. Instead of the thornbush will grow the pine tree, and instead of briers the myrtle will grow. This will be for the Lord's renown, for an everlasting sign, which will not be destroyed" (Isa. 55:11-13). God's

Word always achieves its purpose, and it is for the Lord's eternal glory, not our own. All of creation will sing for him, and there will be joy and peace on earth.

Yes, God favors his children. All can come to God and receive the benefits of his nourishment—not only food but also that which satisfies and delights the soul. He wants a relationship with us. He favors us and wants to bless us, to make us desirable to others by endowing us with splendor. The entire world will want to know God because of the Lord on display in our lives. He wants us to call on him, for he is holy. He reminds us he will achieve his purposes and that there will be joy and peace on earth through him.

A Personal Encounter

"Answer to a Prayer"

I asked for an answer to a prayer

You gave me a dream instead

In that answer you loved me so

I didn't know what I'd asked for

My deepest desire you met with yourself

What I hoped for I got in abundance

You shaped and formed my heart inside

Placed your courage, took away my pride

What an answer to my prayer

You took me by the hand

Walked me through the battleground

So I could know the victory

Now I'm asking to remember

All that you have done

For a grateful heart, one full of praise

To live, to believe, to dream

God is the Author of New Beginnings

> Forget the former things; do not dwell on the past. See,
> I am doing a new thing! Now it springs up; do you not
> perceive it? I am making a way in the desert and streams
> in the wasteland (Isa. 43:18-19).

God promises us newness in our lives, in our hearts, and in our hope for now and eternity. The Isaiah passage refers to what God has planned for his people in Jesus. It also reminds us of what we have in Christ Jesus when we believe in him and believe him.

> Therefore, if anyone is in Christ, he is a new creation; the
> old has gone, the new has come! (2 Cor. 5:17).

When the Holy Spirit dwells in the believer, he or she becomes a new person on the inside. The believer is not the same anymore but is instead a new creation.

> …You have taken off your old self with its practices and
> have put on the new self, which is being renewed in
> knowledge in the image of its Creator (Col. 3:9-10).

Newness is not something we can grasp all at once; it is more a state of becoming. We have only to choose to be new, and with that choice God transforms us. The more we know Christ, the more we are new in him and become like him.

God is the author of new beginnings. Does the old wear us down? Do we feel like we do the same ugly things over and over?

God wants us to forget the former things, not dwell on the past, b turn it over to him so he can change us into his new creation. He will give us a new beginning, authored, planned, and divinely led. We have to choose to believe we can take off the old self and be made new in Christ Jesus. As Ken Boa points out in his Reflections Ministries newsletter (May 2010), "God's promise to you: New life requires only one thing: Faith in my promises."

A NEW DAY

The book of Lamentations tells us that God's mercies renew each day: "Because of the Lord's great love we are not consumed, for his compassions never fail. They are new every morning; great is your faithfulness" (3:22-23). Do we believe that? I sometimes wake with the same disappointments, the same unbelief, and the same grievances. God tells us that we don't have to live that way. We can forgive our neighbor, our friend, our husbands, our children, or our parents. In addition, I am forgiven and can begin anew. I may still be disappointed about things, that is true. Life is full of wrong turns, consequences to our actions we would like to change, and things that are not fair. But I desire newness.

I like new things, new hope, a new start, a new day. Do we take God's Word seriously when we are promised a fresh start and a brand-new day? The Author of Scripture says he will give us a clean slate each time we ask for it. Do we believe we have that kind of forgiveness, and that we don't have to stay in the same old unforgiveness, yesterday's disappointments, and unbelief? Do we grasp the significance of God's new mercies daily? The first thing, perhaps a new thing, is to ask God to forgive us. His Word says that if we ask, it will be given. Then we must believe he has given. "Belief" is essential; we must be convicted that what God says is true. We must

ve *in* God, but we must believe *God*. He is who he says
he does what he says he will do. Are we grateful for
v mercies every morning?

What about disappointments? This world is not perfect, but a
world is coming that will be. God says that there will be a new
heaven and a new earth one day. He also says to pray for his will to
be done on earth as it is in heaven. We are to anticipate this day, and
to know the Bible is clear that "hope does not disappoint us, because
God has poured out his love into our hearts by the Holy Spirit, whom
he has given us" (Rom. 5:5).

In the book of Lamentations Jeremiah says,

> I remember my affliction and my wandering, the bitterness
> and the gall. I well remember them, and my soul is
> downcast within me. Yet this I call to mind and therefore
> I have hope: Because of the Lord's great love we are not
> consumed, for his compassions never fail. They are new
> every morning; great is your faithfulness (3:19-23).

Only God can give us a new day, a fresh start, a clean slate. He
is our hope today and tomorrow. God desires for us to begin anew
at any time of our lives. When we turn to him or cry out to him,
he gives us a new direction. In Isaiah 43: 18-19, the prophet tells
the Israelites to forget their past bondage and focus on God who is
making a way for them: "Forget the former things; do not dwell on
the past. See, I am doing a new thing! Now it springs up; do you
not perceive it? I am making a way in the desert and streams in the
wasteland." The same is true for us today. When we turn to God,
he makes a way for us in our circumstances, whatever they may be.
God is the author of new beginnings.

Isaiah proclaims that God is doing something new in our lives,
and then asks the question, "Do you not perceive it?" The same

question might be put to us: Can't we see it? The newness is in the eye of the beholder. We must *expect* to see God and his work in our lives in order to see them. He is always there, but we must have spiritual hearts to know him, ears to hear him, and eyes to see him.

We must focus on the problem solver, not the problem. God is the problem solver, but more than that, he is author of hope. Even in dire situations, God is aware and in control. When we focus on him, when our hearts, minds, ears, and eyes are set upon him, he clears the way through the deserts and the wastelands.

> Forget the former things; do not dwell on the past. See, I am doing a new thing! Now it springs up; do you not perceive it? I am making a way in the desert and streams in the wasteland (Isa. 43:18-19).

PERSONAL ENCOUNTERS OF NEWNESS

"A New Beginning"

Lonely, afraid, sad

Heartsick bad

Body wasting away

Nothing is the day

Nights long

Pain stays

All is said

What's life-dead

Cry out

Even whisper

Can you hear me

I'm dying

I hear you

I've been waiting

For your call

Day is coming

Light is breaking

Body is awaking

Pain is gone, fear subsides

Somehow brought to the other side

Overwhelming gratitude

Peace besides

Day is waiting

A new beginning

"Create in Me"

Create in me a clean heart, O God

Help me stay focused on you, I pray

Keep me humble and right in your eyes

Evil and bad choices don't allow to be disguised

Create in me compassion

That would grow from a heart like yours

One of love, mercy, and forgiveness

Only you can do this, Lord

Create in me a word that would

Be a kind and gentle one for good

For a soul that's hurting

And a heart that's wounded

Create in me the story

That tells of your love, power, and glory

Of hopes where hurt was, victory where struggle

And peace where there was chaos and strife

Create in me the life anew

Where victory is true

Help me share your good news story

With all the world for your glory

"Your Mercy"

Your mercy, Oh Lord, astounds me

In awe of how you've shown

Your grace through things certain

A small voice of assurance made known

In the uncertain world of busyness

And to do lists overwhelming

Your grace I overlook until

Your kindness and face appear.

In the darkness and in the forgotten

Places I have been where lost

And not so near to You, You bring me

Back to hear your voice.

You bring me back to know your love

And the surety of your forgiveness

You tell me that you know and understand

The journey where I've been

Your mercy, Oh Lord, sustains my soul

Wonder lifts my heart to seek You

And awe bends my knees

Let me praise you always 'til we meet

My song shall be for You, Oh Lord

To tell of your great mercy

For me and all your children

Let us know You and stay at your feet.

"Morning to Night"

Morning comes from the night

Light from the dark

Treasure brought to light

But found in the night

I've come to know what I know

From walking in the dark

With God as my light to show

How to see, what to do, and where to go

When I fall down, He picks me up

Gives me courage to stand

To know Him, love Him, believe He has a plan

Out of the dark, into huge places, spacious ones in His light

I see, know, and believe Him today

Because He has shown me the Way

From burdens, bondage, and a broken heart

He took me in His arms and gave me a fresh start

"There's Newness in the Air"

There's newness in the air
Freshness to the day
May it be ongoing and linger
Just to stay one more day
The excitement of not knowing
Where this path might lead
Will this journey go somewhere
I've worked for and succeeded
The finality of outcomes
When they don't measure up
To my expectations or desires
For the destination better known
Surprise in the making
We think we know the road
A turn occurs; only heaven knows
What pursuit awaits partaking
A life with purpose we desire
Trying to write, live, and dream it
When deep inside us God Himself
A joy immeasurable completes us
God's story unfolds; hope anew
Wakened by change; empowered to do
A new thing better than before
There's newness in the air

God Is Never Done With Us

God comes softly yet powerfully into our hearts. He invites us into his presence, and as we enter in, he persists in his love for us. In his presence, we are changed. How do we change? We are shaped by divine love, mercy, compassion, and truth as we become more like the Divine. As we open our hearts and read his Word, God can create in us a desire to be more like him.

What does the changed heart look like? The heart that is ready to be shaped is willing to listen, hear, and to be in the presence of God. God makes the changes in us—but only if we let him, only if we choose to be there and to hear him.

A willingness to change has at its core a surrender of the human will. Our *free will* makes us who we are. We can choose to hold on to our frailty and our stubbornness, but we can also choose to let go. When we surrender ourselves to the person of God, we give him access to our entire beings, our will, our hearts, and our bodies.

In the Valley

For much of our lives we will have struggles. Sometimes in the real "down" seasons, where we see nothing of hope or promise, we can't make the bad go away. Even with positive outlooks and optimism, the reality is that things are rough. What can we do?

We have to press forward knowing that God is present no matter what our circumstances. He does not want us to suffer, but we do. We will have rough times and terrible circumstances, that is a given, and we do not know how long they will last. What we do know is that the Lord Almighty is always with us, and that his favor lasts a lifetime (Pss. 30, 40). God is present and there when we call on him. As we call, we must hope and *persist* in the knowledge that God is God, and that he does what he says he will do.

What if God is *silent*? What if we cannot hear the Lord when we call? We must still persist and run the race with the hope and knowledge that he will answer. "I am still confident of this: I will see the goodness of the Lord in the land of the living. Wait for the Lord; be strong and take heart and wait for the Lord" (Ps. 27:13-14). In fact, God probably already has answered. He may be saying *wait a bit*, or *no way*, or *ask for something bigger*. In any event, God does what he says he will do and God is who he says he is.

We have times of not surrendering to God, but that does not mean he ever leaves us. That will never happen. We may not believe him during the rough times, and we may not even seek him, but he is not done with us. In the valley or on the mountaintop, we may wander from the path, yet he does not forsake us. He is not done.

THE LIFE WE CHOOSE

Just as we enjoy being around those we love and those who love us, God wants us to be around him. He delights in us. The psalmist says God "brought me out into a spacious place; he rescued me because he delighted in me" (Ps. 18:19). God is in the darkness and in the light, and he brings light to the deep and lonely places. Nothing is hidden from him. And when it serves God's purposes, he reveals hidden things to us, as the prophet Daniel wrote: "He reveals deep and hidden things; he knows what lies in darkness, and light dwells with him" (Dan. 2:22). Wherever we are is where God will meet us. The more we open our hearts and minds to him, the more he comes. He will never force himself on us but will wait until we invite him in.

Choosing life that embraces the triune God is a decision we must make in order to live a life connected to the Absolute source of life. If we choose to ask him into our lives, there is no question that he will come. Joining in fellowship with him on a continual basis becomes more and more a reality. It is in showing up and meeting him that we will know him and experience him in our lives.

I have not always seen God in my life or known he was there, and I assume this is true of many believers. But he was there, and he is there. The story of God in my life is one of struggle that has led ultimately and entirely to hope. People disappoint. Circumstances do, too. And so do things. But God does not disappoint. Seeing God's hand in my life today and throughout my journey has been the greatest joy I have ever experienced. One thing I have learned is that God is never done with us.

GOD AND THE FIRST TWENTY-FIVE YEARS

God has always been there for me, and I have known this ever since I was a little girl. Even though I knew he was present, I did not always act like he was. My childhood was lonely and I was fearful about a lot of things. At an early age God gave me good intuition for discerning what was true and what was not. I knew things about my mother and the family situation that troubled me. Things she said to me or things I heard often just did not ring true. Even so, I started doubting myself because if I did not believe what my mother said was true, this was tantamount to judging her and putting her in a bad light. I didn't want to do that. But if I had believed God gave me the gift of discernment, I would have been a lot less fearful about things.

There were other things that kept me in a perpetual state of doubt. My mother did not like me. I believe she loved me in her own limited way (I believe that now, but I did not think so as I was growing up). She ridiculed me and kept me in a state of shame. I always felt less about myself when she spoke to me or interacted with me in other ways. Trust issues became a real problem, for I frankly did not trust her, and I didn't like myself for feeling that way. As I grew older, I would wonder what girl in the world would doubt that her own mother loved her. Of course, I did not really think about it much because to do so would have been too painful. What I did think about was what she said to me and to others that was usually not very nice. For her I was too sensitive. Too moody. Too fat. Too smart. Too perfectionistic. "Where did this come from?" she would say.

God was certainly present in my life. I remember at age three being in the car and waiting for my mother from choir practice and saying to my father "Here comes God and God's mother," pointing to the minister and his wife. The minister thought it was the highest compliment of his life. His wife, not so much. At nine, during a Billy Graham crusade on television, I gave my life to Christ. I knelt by the bed and asked Christ into my life. Things really didn't seem that different, except I knew that I had done it. It was my act, my commitment, and I did not share it with anyone in my family for fear they would laugh at me. Later, I was confirmed in the church where I grew up.

God was in my life when I went to a new high school and didn't know anybody. I was a good student and thrived on making good grades, and so school became my new place of security. In God's providence he provided several teachers who knew me and loved me. My high school Bible teacher was a real inspiration to me and encouraged me, and my piano teacher loved me and inspired me to bigger things.

Still building walls of protection because I had trouble trusting, I was not sure of myself in relationships. I made friends, but not very many and not very easily. One family in particular was my safe haven. They invited me to places where I met many godly and

Bible-focused young men and women. There were times when I let my guard down, but not often. I felt safe when I was studying or doing something academic. God provided safety all long, but I did not know in my heart that I was safe.

I was at a new low when I went off to college. Without the underpinnings of my family and a firm foundation spiritually, I was really scared and anything but confident in my abilities. This was painful because, up until that time, I was very secure in my academic success. The fears were now about money and being able to support myself. I had been told often I needed to earn money to be self-supporting. I paid my way through college with scholarships and part-time work, and that gave me a great feeling of accomplishment. Through the fears God was there, even when I got sick during my sophomore year. He came to my rescue and delivered me to a better place spiritually. I began talking to God, even though I admit it might have been only to petition him for a better path of hope.

I needed to make decisions about majors and perhaps transferring schools. It was then that I knew that God was clear about his intentions for me—that I stay where I was. After this became clear, several professors came through for me and helped me develop a path for graduation and graduate school. God made himself known when I cried out to him.

In graduate school the Lord provided me with a godly friend in my program. We were able to work in the same area and take classes together; I felt safe again while working on my masters' degree. Then all you-know-what came apart, as life sometimes does. Many things happened at once to prove devastating for me. I became deathly ill and many of my health care providers thought I would not make it, including me. Once again God made himself known and brought me through miraculously. I had been given a new lease on life, but

I was unable to work for a while and now graduate school was not financially feasible. Soon after, I failed the comprehensive exams, which was soul-crushing for me. I was at the end of myself physically, mentally, and emotionally. I not only had to deal with academic and financial issues, but my family of origin had been with me day and night for weeks and were nearly driving me crazy. Fear set in like no other time. Still, God is faithful and he was there in his Word. For the first time in my life, in graduate school, the Bible became my source of strength. At the time I needed the divine nudge the most, he was there. Having to drop out of school and start working was an extraordinary setback, but God set me on my feet and gave me a fresh start.

I began going to a new church regularly and met a fine group of young single men and women who became my circle of friends during this time. In this church I found solid fellowship with God's people while being nourished in his Word. God was in my life in a bigger and better way. Yet, I was still fearful and unsettled about what was in store for me. I knew it had to be good, but I doubted myself and whether I was good enough for it. God was drawing me to him once again.

I met my husband of thirty-plus years in the Sunday school class of the new church, and we married in this church with the friends we made in this class. God brought me to the graduate program and allowed me the many hardships to bring me back to him and to provide my soul mate for life. I was beginning to understand God's favor in a new light, even though I had glimpsed it many times before.

God took us to another state for my husband to start graduate school. Because I had started working in a secondary school setting while I was doing graduate work, my boss in the current job recommended me for a permanent position on the new college campus. This allowed me to continue working on my master's degree while my husband did his. And God did not stop providing there. A woman who had taken me under her wing from our church in the college town knew a professor in my field who needed house sitters and asked us if we would like to do it. What a huge thing for newlyweds living in a tiny on-campus apartment. We felt wealthy beyond comparison. We even had all of our immediate and extended families for Thanksgiving that year. God was showering his favor on us in ways I could not refute …husband, home, church, graduate school, and work. Our favorite early memories were of those years. We had fun learning about each other and making new friends as a couple. We had a small group of friends of all ages who went out once a week after my choir practice, so our first church memories together were wonderful.

I knew God is good and that he provides for the faithful, but I still had walls of protection up from my early years. I feared letting my husband down; I wanted to please him and yet I mostly feared intimacy (and didn't know it at the time). He came from a family where everyone tried to be perfect and measure up. We were both in the mode of accomplishing, but our goals were different. My husband was accomplishing for his father and for himself, while I was accomplishing for my husband and myself. Walls go up when a couple's goals go off in different directions, and this creates separation as well as protection from each other. If that goes on for any length of time, it is not good for a relationship with each other or with God. Still, God knew us and gave us to each other, and we often marvel at his humor and his sovereignty in choosing us for one another.

GOD AND THE SECOND TWENTY-FIVE YEARS

The first four years of marriage were exhilarating and soulful and fun. Because we were both searching for significance in different places, the next four years were spent gaining more education and more success independent from one another. I knew God was there, but I was not leaning on the truth from his Word. For me, it became a time of running from God—not consciously, but in practice. I wanted to be loved more than anything, and the only way I knew how to accomplish this was to be successful. God knew differently and waited patiently for me. He provided another excellent graduate program, and another master's degree. He also placed us in my husband's home city for work and success and our first home in the suburbs. If this was not enough, I landed my dream job, one of the original team in a startup software company. Yet these things did not make me happy; I was on a treadmill of my own making and working harder than I ever had in my life. My husband was a good provider and soul mate, but he was on his own journey, full of promise and future success.

Our first pregnancy was a miscarriage. Then my father died. My father was the only one in my family who really knew me and loved me for who I was while growing up. He was our rock; his faith was solid, and his hope was secure in Christ. How could God let him die at the young age of fifty-seven? I visited him every weekend the year before he died. But to my mind it was ultimately a betrayal by God to let my father die and not save him from the cancer.

Our second pregnancy went all the way to full-term, including my daughter's birth right on the due date. God was ever present during the months prior to her birth and during the labor and delivery. She was magnificent, more than I could ever have dreamed. As I went back to work part-time from home, I felt full but fearful again. Why was this happening? I thought maybe I was just plain ungrateful and selfish. There were deeper issues: God does not leave us alone but is always drawing us closer to himself. When our daughter was two-and-a-half years old, I began wondering if she would grow up knowing I loved her. The fear of my daughter not knowing I loved her became overwhelming, and actual obsession with me. God works in mysterious ways. As I prayed for her, I began searching for God's truth in his Word. At the same time, my work became a burden and I found myself viewing all of life in a different way. Why was I so driven to do everything on the list, just to do everything on the list again? It seems there was a void inside of me. But God knew the void could only be filled with his love. I knew all of this intellectually and I thought I really knew it in my heart as well. But God knows me better than I do myself. He knows every detail of my past, my present, and my future, and he wants me to know him as well as he knows me.

I was walking in our neighborhood when God spoke to me to say my daughter knew I loved her. And this was the beginning of my journey to knowing fully that God loved me, too. In First John 4:16 we read, "And so we know and rely on the love God has for us. God is love. Whoever lives in love lives in God, and God in him." I remember when I realized that God really loved *me*. I was in the home of my youth where I had felt unloved and dismissed. God was showing me he loved me then, now, and forever. Coming to terms with God really loving me was a breakthrough of proportions that only God knows. He wanted me to know his love myself. I stepped out on faith and made a conscious decision to believe that I was loved by the God of the universe. That small seed of faith blossomed into an adventure of faith I could have never dreamed possible.

While the layers are thick in these walls of protection, one thin layer after another vanishes as we choose to believe. Will we choose to believe now? What about next time, or the time after that? God is faithful. What we need to do is make a step of faith; when we do, he multiplies the distance. We decide to take the rough road, and God makes the rough one smooth. He is never done with us. If we surrender to him, he binds up our brokenness and sets our captive hearts free, the way he did with the prophet Isaiah:

> The Spirit of the Sovereign Lord is on me, because the Lord has anointed me to proclaim good news to the poor. He has sent me to bind up the brokenhearted, to proclaim freedom for the captives and release from darkness for the prisoners, to proclaim the year of the Lord's favor and the day of vengeance of our God, to comfort all who mourn, and provide for those who grieve in Zion—to bestow on them a crown of beauty instead of ashes, the oil of joy instead of mourning, and a garment of praise instead of a spirit of despair. They will be called oaks of righteousness, a planting of the Lord for the display of his splendor. They will rebuild the ancient ruins and restore the places long devastated; they will renew the ruined cities that have been devastated for generations (Isa. 61:1-4).

We can choose to believe that he can set us free. In my case, I had to know the Truth in order to know which things are lies. The accusations and the condemnation I felt and feared were not from God, and I had to learn that. He was bringing this to light as I studied God's divine revelation in the Bible. He lovingly took one untruth at a time and showed me how it was not biblical. I was his child and the daughter of the King. He would not withhold any good thing from me—or any of his legitimate children. I believed in him, and now I believe him at his Word and in his Word.

GUIDING US TO A SPACIOUS PLACE

King David wrote, "You have not given me into the hands of the enemy but have set my feet in a spacious place" (Ps. 31:8). A few years ago, I felt the urge to check into other schools for my children. It was not a high probability that we would move them; yet, it seemed like the right thing to do. God was urging me to open my eyes to what he would have for them. As I went to an open house, I was drawn to the Psalm 31:8 Scripture that God had placed on my heart that morning. It seemed as though God whispered to me that he was guiding our family to a spacious place if I would just trust him to do it. I did trust him, although not without doubt, questioning, or unbelief. But I had done this before, and God had given me the biggest gift of my life: belief in his love for me. The journey involved so many parts of our lives and the lives of our children. But God had been preparing each of our hearts for this, and while I knew the road was a difficult one, I also knew it was an unavoidable one if we wanted what God had planned for us. I came before him every morning in prayer to know him and his heart for each of us, and, most urgently, for guidance and leading on where he wanted us to go. In this time, my faith grew in ways unimaginable to me. The Word of God was truly being written on my heart, which was truly becoming a heart of faith.

He moved us across the river to a spacious place. My daughter would be in a larger high school, and my son would be in a small elementary school down the street. We would live in a real neighborhood, with children close by for my son to play with. My husband could work from a home office with plenty of space and privacy. As for me, I knew God had already set my feet in a spacious place by creating the spacious place in my heart. The whole ordeal was truly amazing and life changing, physically, emotionally, and spiritually.

God delivers us to the place he has chosen for us to be whom we were created to be. We knew we had been delivered to be free to hope and dream as heaven's sons and daughters. Shortly after we moved into the neighborhood, I was walking and noticed stonework in many yards. I began thinking about how we had crossed the river to a spacious place when I thought about the story of the Israelites journey across the Jordan River to Gilgal, the account of which is told in the fourth chapter of the Old Testament book of Joshua. God told them to "choose twelve men from among the people, one from each tribe, and tell them to take up twelve stones from the middle of the Jordan, from right where the priests are standing, and carry them over with you and put them down at the place where you stay tonight.... These stones are to be a memorial to the people of Israel forever" (Josh. 4:2-3, 7). Strange as it may seem, I felt God was telling me to place stones in our yard to remind us of our journey. Just as I felt the urge to do this, I remembered another Scripture where Christ says that the stones will cry out if we don't praise him. "'I tell you,' he replied, 'if they keep quiet, the stones will cry out'" (Luke 19:40). And so, as a sign of God's faithfulness and goodness to us, we have memorial stones in our front yard to symbolize God's truth, our trust in him, and the freedom he gives that is like no other. We praise him for setting our feet in a spacious place, and just as the Israelites were instructed to tell their children their stories and remind them of God's faithfulness through the generations, our stones will remind us of the same thing. And we will tell our faith story to the generations.

The Lord is making me freer and freer and removing more and more layers of protection from me as I exercise deeper belief in him. Each set is a step of faith, but God is propelling me in the direction of faith and freedom, trusting him and letting go of what hinders me from running the race marked out for me (Heb. 12:1). He is merciful and gracious and does not allow me to see more than I can handle at any given time. The really painful and hard issues he brings to the surface in the most loving manner. I know by the manner in which things surface now whether or not they come from God. It will be an urging or something so radical or removed from my thought life that I know it is from God's heart. Then whoa, I've got to go on the journey, because it will be the ride of my life and the most freeing one.

QUESTIONS TO PONDER

Looking back, were there times in your life when you knew God was there?

If you have not placed your trust in God, are you willing to ask him to enter your life and take control of it? If you do so, he will show up! And he will comfort you with his love and presence in your life. In the gospel of Matthew Jesus says, "Surely I am with you always, to the very end of the age" (28:20).

What does love always do? In First Corinthians Paul tells us that love "always protects, always trusts, always hopes, always perseveres" (13:7).

God Continually Invites Us to Come to Him

I want to be thirsty for God. In Isaiah chapter fifty-five, the invitation goes out to all who are thirsty: "Come, all you who are thirsty, come to the waters; and you who have no money, come, buy and eat! Come, buy wine and milk without money and without cost" (55:1). Though our needs are met without cost, we are not always thirsty for God and what he offers. The best times of my life have been in the Lord's presence with his guidance, but I tend to forget that unless he places me in situations I don't know how to solve or get through on my own. And isn't that exactly the human condition? We forget we can't attain the abundant life from the position of the human condition. That takes God. I don't want to live in the human condition when Christ offers me life that is abundant. If I stay in his Word and on my knees, I am equipped to hear him and go through the day, whatever it entails. When I don't, I try making it through on my own. That is a recipe for trouble and being in over my head.

The most dangerous condition is the satisfied life where one is spiritually dulled to the fact that Christ is alive and can give a higher and more fulfilled life complete with freedom, hope, and mercy. We have all seen people who are not thirsty for more because they think they have it all. They are insensitive to life on a higher plane because to them life is only about certain more down-to-earth things, such as family, possessions, vacations, and retirement. Or they are hyped by possessions, achievements, or the next big deal, luxury vacation, or dream home. But again, these are human approaches to life. There is nothing bad about any of these things, but when one is dead to the fact that the Creator is alive and can give abundantly more in a relationship with him, one's life seeks the low ebb. It may be living, but it is not a life.

The prophet Isaiah was especially profound in this way. He didn't tell us to wait until we needed the Lord before looking for him. He said, "Seek the Lord while he may be found; call on him while he is near. Let the wicked forsake their ways and the unrighteous their thoughts. Let them turn to the Lord, and he will have mercy on them, and to our God, for he will freely pardon" (55:6-7). Isaiah made it clear that God is always looking for us, and he is always present with us. We just have to call on him and we need to be thirsty for the life that only he can give. Calling on God for a "fix" instead of for what he offers us is not the way to go. If we will receive what he offers, it is better than what we thought we needed. God knows us from the inside out; our needs and our desires are no secret to him. He created us with the spiritual need, and only God will fill this need. If we go looking for nourishment elsewhere, it will never satisfy.

"Seek the Lord while he may be found; call on him while he is near," is the advice Isaiah give us. Even though God is merciful in his invitation to come, he wants us to search for him and to come while he is near. This means we are to come when he draws us in, not wait until we find it convenient.

One might ask, "What if I am not thirsty?" We will all be thirsty one day. And when we are, what part of our lives would we change? What part of our past would we like to cut off? What would our futures entail that we are not prepared to handle? Have we always had what we wanted or needed? When we realize that God wants to handle these things in our lives, being thirsty is a good thing. It propels us to desire more, to want God more, and to hope for a stronger relationship with the One and Only who died and rose again so we can hope and heal and spend eternity together with him.

God invites us to come and, as it turns out, it is the invitation of a lifetime.

GOD DRAWS US TO HIMSELF

> Before they call I will answer; while they are still speaking
> I will hear (Isa. 65:24).

How many have asked themselves, "How did I get here? How did I wind up at this juncture in my life?" It is a question we have all asked because sometimes we are in a situation that is just not what we expected or wanted it to be. Maybe we have been running wildly and wanting to stop, or to have someone else take over. Maybe we prayed that God would help us with something particularly difficult and things are not getting any easier. Perhaps something just doesn't ring true and there is a desire for the real thing. In all situations, trying or otherwise, God is wooing us. Whenever we seek something to fill the void, God is calling out to us. That is the way we are made, and God is the only one who can fill our void. While he will not force himself on us, he keeps using our circumstances in life to draw us back.

It would be impossible to name the myriad of ways God in his infinite wisdom and love calls us back. We cannot fathom the mind of God, and we will never be able to determine why, how, or what the Father will do to discipline, protect, or lead his children. But he gives us minds and hearts to choose to do things God's way.

Stumbling blocks and life questions, which are universal in nature, can lead us back to God, our Creator and Savior. He gives us hearts to know him and the desires deep within that can only be met by him. Sometimes, when we reach the end of ourselves, we cry out to find the Savior has been there all along, wooing and waiting for us to call.

Our Lack Brings us Back

A little girl, now a grown woman whom we will call Caron, says she knew things, especially emotional things, as a small child at home:

> I sensed sadness, depression, and neediness in the people around me. Deep things surrounded me, and although I didn't want to notice them, I did. Through the years, I experienced a lot of pain because I cared about whether a person was happy or not. If it helped for me to please them, I wanted to do so. When a person knows you care too much about what they feel, and they are not honorable

in their relationships, they can use your caring against you by asking of you things they have no business asking. My refusal to do the things asked of me led to accusations and dismissal. Thus, I began trusting people less and less because of the rejection I feared by not doing the things asked of me. Violated by manipulation at an early age, I began a difficult journey of distrusting people and my own relationship skills. But I had seen some good models in my extended family and in my church community who seemed to have hope, love, and joy in their lives. I knew I wanted what they had.

Caron knew she lacked real love in her life. She was too young to have the skills in relationships that she needed to cope in many situations, but she was emotionally savvy enough to know that manipulating people was not right. The relationships in her home were not what they were supposed to be, and she wanted what she had seen but knew she didn't have. Out of her lack, she was searching—even as a small girl—for the very thing that would give her hope, love, and joy in her life. She wanted significance, worth, and relationship. She was seeking God, who had given her a God-shaped desire for his love and protection. Her lack brought her back.

Our Stuff is Not Enough

Sometimes it is not the lack of things we have but rather the things themselves that bring us back to God. This is especially true when we realize that things are not enough. After a dinner party that she has just given, Mary was pondering her feelings:

I was up in my bedroom after a successful dinner party for my husband's client, and going over the evening in my mind. My two children were in their beds in our beautiful home in a lovely neighborhood. My loving husband was finishing up some work in his study. I had everything I ever wanted: a husband who loves me, children we adore, and a wonderful home. What is wrong with me to question and to want something more? I just felt so empty inside. I cried out to God, "Help me; I am so empty and alone."

Mary's dreams for herself came true, but they fell short of satisfying her. Her stuff was not enough. There was still a void in her life, and she knew it. She cried out to God for help. Did he hear her? Isaiah 65:24 says, "Before they call I will answer; while they are still speaking I will hear." God answers before we call and he hears while we are crying out to him. God knows our every need before we do.

BETRAYAL AND DISAPPOINTMENT

We don't know where else to turn. Everyone in our lives has proven to be untrustworthy. We don't even see ourselves as trustworthy. A betrayal is like a death in that after the betrayal the old relationship is not viable anymore. Where do we go when we cannot trust?

Disappointments happen in relationships in marriage, school, work, church, with our dreams, and in all aspects of life. Everything and everyone has the potential to disappoint us, including ourselves. I believe that there is a desire deep inside everyone to trust in someone or something that is greater than ourselves. Only God does not disappoint, as the apostle Paul reminds us in Romans 5:5: "Now hope does not disappoint, because the love of God has been poured out in our hearts by the Holy Spirit who was given to us" (NJKV).

Will God draw us to himself when we are betrayed or disappointed by others or by ourselves? Yes, he answers us even before we cry out. In Romans 5:3-4, Paul tells us that "we also rejoice in our sufferings, because we know that suffering produces perseverance; perseverance, character; and character, hope." It is this hope that will not disappoint.

God knows us better than we know ourselves, and remarkably he loves us anyway. As a Father, he desires our closeness, our attention, and our devotion. He does not want to lose or be estranged from any one of his children, and he will do anything to save us, including sacrificing his only Son Jesus.

SUMMARY

God loved us first, as we see described in Scripture. While we make the choice to reciprocate his love, God is responsible for drawing us to himself. We do not and cannot come on our own. We read in the gospel of John, "This is why I told you that no one can come to me unless the Father has enabled him" (6:65). When we do return to God, we are returning to the One who created us and loves us with an everlasting love. It is only through this relationship with God the Father in Jesus Christ the Son that the chasm in our being will be filled.

As God fills us, we want to know him better, and so he continues to use the relationship with us to transform us into who he created us to be. He chooses to see us as he sees Jesus, as perfect sons and daughters. God takes what we offer him and makes it in the image of his Son, so that we become like him in the process. "Now we are children of God, and what we will be has not yet been made known. But we know that when he appears, we shall be like him, for we shall see him as he is" (1 John 3:2). In other words, will know him when we see him (in heaven) because we will look like him. What a great

God who would create us to participate in his marvelous purpose and plan here on planet Earth. We only have to be willing to love and surrender our lives to the Lord, lives we cannot keep anyway. He does the rest; he loves us, draws us to himself, and in the process transforms us into persons like him. And then he takes us home. During the journey with trials and temptations, it is the ride of all rides, complete with riches stored in secret places, revealed mysteries, and promises of freedom, joy, and wholeness.

It all begins with God and it all ends with him. And everything in between, well …that is God, too.

DEEP CALLS TO DEEP

The psalmist said "deep calls to deep in the roar of your waterfalls; all your waves and breakers have swept over me" (Ps. 42:7). Deep calls to deep. Within each of us is the desire to know the unfathomable God, the one who knows and sees us for who we are. If we look deep inside, we recognize that we both fear this God and we love him. We fear him and run from him because we want to be free to live independently and to be our own guides in life. Some of us are ashamed of what we have done with or in our lives, and so we want to hide. Some of us can't stop doing things to hurt ourselves or others, our lives are in a mess, and we don't even want God to know us. But he does know us and he loves us still. Deep calls to deep because that is how the Creator made us, with deep souls to be loved by an everlasting Father, the Creator of heaven and earth. The Father loves us with an unfailing love, no matter what we have done or not done to deserve it.

However far or wide we run, we will not outrun the Father, who is forever drawing us to himself. He will allow us to run and to choose him or not, but his love is so big he would not ever force us into a relationship with him. He is there all the time, but he is not intruding or barging his way into places we do not want him. He just keeps pursuing. And if we decide to ask him into our lives, he will come.

Deep calls to deep because we want the deepest parts of ourselves to be touched and to be known fully and understood and loved in spite of it all. Jesus loves us and understands in a way no other can or will. It is deep and true and forever.

DEEP WITHIN

I heard Jesus on my walk today when I was thinking about a person who really hurts me over and over again. He said to love her like no one else can. He reminded me that because she hurts me, I know something about her and can pray for her uniquely. This evening I saw Jesus at a business dedication, and his presence was as real as the people I spoke to who were starting a new venture to the glory of God. When my son told me a quote he had heard today, I heard the voice of Jesus in him. Some days I miss hearing and seeing the Lord because I am too busy doing or talking and not listening.

There is a place deep within me that has been crying out lately. It is not sad, exactly, but it is real, and it is sometimes dark and sometimes light. When I notice it, I am more alive, more aware of life and what is going on around me.... the unseen things, too. When I acknowledge the moment, my eyes brim with tears; I want to let go and surrender. I know that God is present and he is revealing things to me in my deepest self. He is deep within, and I am on the mountaintop looking at his back. I want more of him.

God comes deep within to anyone willing to say, "Come, Lord Jesus." He is present and real and wants to have a close relationship with all his children.

God Rescues Us from Trouble to Safety

> You have not handed me over to the enemy but have set
> my feet in a spacious place (Ps. 31:8). .

Have you ever had a time in your life when you didn't really know how you got from one place to another, and you were really relieved not to be where you had been? I know that God has delivered me from situations that were too difficult for me. He has a way of picking us up and carrying us to safety when we are in over our heads. But that doesn't always happen. We might wonder on occasion why the Lord did not come to our rescue in difficult circumstances where we needed a way out. I don't know why he does that at times. But I do know that God will not allow harm for his children, those who faithfully follow him. He will not allow us to be harmed spiritually by Satan, our accuser. The Enemy has no power over God's beloved.

In my mind's eye I picture God picking up his dear one and taking them to safety and setting them down in a place to roam and be free to do and be who God has designed them to be. This is not unlike a mother who sees her child in danger and picks her up and takes her to a place she can play and be free to be a child in a protected spot. I remember when my son was not quite two years old, when he loved to go to a small neighborhood lake and feed the ducks. This particular afternoon the geese were out in numbers. My son thought that it was really a sight to see and he went running after a rather large gander that was actually bigger than he was. As the goose was about to take a chunk out of my son's finger, I scooped him up in my arms and ran to the playground nearby. I was quite relieved that my son really didn't have time to think about what had just happened. I had taken him from harm into a safer and freer environment to play and be a toddler with a lot of energy to roam and have fun.

God carries us at times when he knows we are either dead-set on a harmful situation or when do not have the strength to carry on. He knows his sheep and will not allow them to wander too far in a bad spot. We can count on divine protection and guidance, especially when we have lost our way and are going in a harmful direction.

God enjoys his creation. He sees us through the blood of Christ and declares us righteous and pure and blameless. When we surrender and allow God's deliverance, he carries us to the other side of the Jordan to a resting place and his inheritance. We come into his confidence, his own, a sweet knowing of his mercy and love. It is when we recognize his undeserved yet freely given grace at this time in this place that we acknowledge our neediness for him and receive the remarkable, yet unfathomable God of the universe. It is then we are wildly free of the past circumstances or strongholds and new to this life of freedom in a place of our own with God.

I believe that in this deliverance God gives us a new name. If we ask, he will tell us what it is. Yet it is in his name that we have newness, not in our own. Our own new name, however, reminds us of the intimacy of God in our lives. We have authority and power in him who gave us deliverance and set us free from our past. We can be bold in his name. When we share our story with others, we are reminding our brothers and sisters of God's faithfulness and mercy, but we are also telling others of the richness and sovereignty of God in this world. Christ is the glory of God on earth, and we are to be light and message-bearers now and in the future.

When God delivers us, he makes his covenant known to us as the psalmist says in Psalm 25:14: "The Lord confides in those who fear him; he makes his covenant known to them." It is an intimate relationship with the God of the universe sharing himself with us. Hallelujah! God reveals himself to us through trials, through his Word, through prayer, through our relationships, and through our resting in his presence. In all of these things he teaches us about himself.

From Child of Woe to Woman of Freedom

> You turned my wailing into dancing; you removed my sackcloth and clothed me with joy, that my heart may sing to you and not be silent. O Lord my God, I will give you thanks forever (Ps. 30:11-12).

When one fails to mature into an adult, the years keep adding up but the maturity and wisdom do not follow. We have all seen older women still acting like adolescents with their temper tantrums to get their way. Or middle-aged men still using their muscle strength or power plays to get their way in a business interaction. It may seem comical, but it is tragic and sad.

When I became an adult in years I still had a lot of growing up to do. In real life, I was an adult most of my life when I was actually a child. I cooked, cleaned the house, took care of younger siblings, and made the peace in my family. That is certainly adult work for a child of nine or ten. My family actually called me the maid when I came home from college, a joke with too much truth in it to be amusing. I believe the reason I became an adult with a lot of growing up to do was that I had handled so many adult things at a young age that I had not had the time to grow normally, to learn and deal with feelings and emotional maturity. Because I had not dealt with how I felt about most things, I was still a little girl, full of pent up anger and hate—mostly towards myself.

I couldn't escape the bad things I thought of myself and said to myself. On the outside I looked like a normal young girl who had dreams, aspirations, intelligence, and heart. I really cared about others because I knew how to do that; I had been doing that for years.

Yet I didn't know how to care for *me*, or how to let someone else do it, either. There was no frame of reference for it. So I was stuck in depression and despair, and the only way out was to work really hard and care for others really well. This seemed to work for me for a while, that is until it didn't work anymore.

I was a young mother in a decade-long marriage with a really high-pressured career in a startup software company. Things were going well for me, and I was a dedicated workaholic. I cared deeply about my marriage, and I cared deeply about my new daughter and what I was teaching her about life and family. I also cared about how my husband and I balanced our careers. I had not come to terms with my depression or despair, but I was superb at doing the things on my list, no matter how the list kept on going and growing. What if my daughter grew up and never realized I loved her? I asked this question of myself over and over. Where did this question come from? I didn't know the answer, but I did know I wanted her to know more than anything that I loved her. This fact became the beginning of a new faith journey for me and my family. The child of woe in me didn't want my daughter having a child of woe as a mother. I knew the answer depended on me.

My prayer was a simple one: "God, change me." And he does change us when we ask. He changed my heart's desire, not just to please others in order for them to love me, not just to work hard to mask the pain from not knowing the love of self or others, *but* to love God with all of my heart, mind, soul, and strength, and then to love others and *myself*. I received the love he had for me all along. He made me know his love for me with my heart, instead of just my head. My heart changed when I received his love, and so did the course of my life and my children's lives forever. So began the journey of the child of woe to the woman of freedom.

When one masks pain for a long time, there are many layers to be peeled away. God has been merciful with me by showing me little by little how to pray and work through the junk in my past that has had a way of creeping into the present. He has allowed more pain to face issues and let go of things long gone. But he has never done this by leaving me without his presence, love, and strength every step of the way. Much of my pain lies in the relationships with the family where I was raised. I have been bound by bad and hurtful words from long ago, as well as from words as recent as yesterday. But God is the author of freedom and victory, and he does not want me in slavery to anything or any other. Just as he brought the Israelites out of Egypt, he wants to bring me and each one of us out of our own bondage.

Slavery and bondage come in many forms. It can be a personal thing, such as an addiction. It can also be a familial bondage, such as generations of abuse. But slavery can be something seemingly as simple as doing things the traditional way because "that's the way we have always done it." God wants us to break away from our own traditions to follow his direction. He wants our whole hearts because he is a jealous God who demands our undivided attention. When we give him our hearts, he gives us his life and freedom. Bound by many things, I was a pleaser and caregiver, a workaholic and an anorexic. For generations my family was bound by depression, abuse, and mental illness. We had so many needs not apparent to the outside world that our family became a vacuum instead of a respite. In order to survive in the family, one had to take on the needs of everyone else. Before long, one would be sucked into the sickness of it all and become part of the problem.

When I left to go to graduate school, my mother sent my emotionally ill sister to live with me. It didn't work out, of course, and no one in the family was happy about it. I felt I had failed her and everyone else. I became deathly ill a few months later, surviving in spite of my mother's efforts to keep me from going to the emergency room. In an effort to fill the void in me and mask the pain I felt when I faced myself, I worked hard to achieve a master's degree, and later I earned another master's degree. When I married my husband, my siblings said that I had escaped. They all claimed that my husband was the reason for my success in life. What about all the academic work I did, or the pain I had endured? Did they not count for something? I was bound by their words and their lack of approval. I was bound by a lack of love for myself. I knew it deep inside, and I did not know what to do about it. God knew. He was allowing me to get to the end of myself before starting to rebuild. And the end of myself was coming soon.

My son was a toddler and I was a stay-at-home mom when my brother became severely mentally ill. This was a devastating blow to me because we had been so close most of my life. He now telephoned me nonstop to accuse me of setting him up, spying on him, and other more hideous things. For a couple of years I prayed, called doctors, regularly visited him, and had him come to see me. It became evident my brother needed to go back to his hometown to receive medical help, and my doctor set up appointments with a highly recommended psychiatrist. The new psychiatrist even called my brother at my home to talk and set up appointments with him. When my family heard that I had sent my brother back to his home, they were furious with me and condemned my actions and said terrible accusatory things because I had not kept him in my home to take care of him. I did all I could in my situation, but my brother himself said I had failed in helping him because he did not like the new doctor and did not remain in his care. My brother could not stay in my home because my son was so young and affected by my brother's erratic behavior, as were my daughter, husband, and I. This became my wakeup call for help of my own. I no longer could deal with my family of origin, and I wanted to flee them forever. If I could have, I would have moved to another country without leaving them a number or a forwarding address.

What happened after this really led to the breakthrough of my spiritual journey, for I became free of the strongholds and lies that characterized the culture of the family in which I grew up. God placed a desire in my heart to know him and his Word. As I studied the Bible, God wrote his Truth on my heart. The condemnation I felt for myself and from my family was replaced by his assurance that "therefore, there is now no condemnation for those who are in Christ Jesus" (Rom. 8:1). Living under the threat that I had to please others or my life was in vain was replaced by the knowledge that the only one I had to please was God—and that he loved me enough to die for me whether I pleased him or not. His best was far greater than I could imagine. God was so good to me during this period of time. The fears I held all of my life, and the walls I placed to keep myself safe from things, came tumbling down. Fear was replaced by hope and faith in God and his love for me. Surely there were days when this all seemed greater than I could handle, but I knew by then that the heavenly Father was there to protect and to guide. I had new faith in him.

QUESTIONS TO PONDER

What is your sorrow? Is it addiction, or fear of failure?

Do you want to be rescued from this sorrow? Do you want to change? God wants to take the sorrow from you and replace it with joy and freedom. He wants to heal you, to clothe you with joy so you will tell others about his goodness and love. As the psalmist wrote: "You turned my wailing into dancing; you removed my sackcloth and clothed me with joy, that my heart may sing to you and not be silent. O Lord my God, I will give you thanks forever" (Ps. 30:11-12). .

Pray the simple prayer, "God, change me." When we cry out to him, he answers.

"Free to Be"

I'm free to be

The girl you see

I'm no longer hidden

By doubt, guilt-ridden

He hates this fact

It ruins his act

He had a tight hold

A life, a stronghold

He keeps coming back

Lies, deceit his tact

He cannot have his stay

No room for his way

Broken chains, wounded heart healed

Victory won, Word firmly planted

It won't be recanted; little girl free to know

God's best to live, to grow.

"Free"

I can't see God

but I know His son, Jesus.

He guides me by the Holy Spirit

and teaches me through His word.

I don't understand His ways

or think like He does,

but I know the Savior loves me

which is grace and truth.

Mystery revealed in the Son of the most high

For them to see and for us to believe.

I'm a daughter of the King

A royal robe instead of sackcloth and ashes.

Credited with righteousness-gift beyond compare

For all who believe and receive it-a spacious place and eternal life,

Freedom to be who He created us to be

A child of the King, favored and blessed by God.

I'm a daughter of the King.

I was brokenhearted, and He bound me up.

When in the dark, He made me see.

I was imprisoned and in chains; He set me free.

He gave me a new name; He calls me Victor.

God is in the Hard Stuff

God calls us by name:

I will give you the treasures of darkness, riches stored in
secret places, so that you may know that I am the Lord, the
God of Israel, who summons you by name. (Isa. 45:3).

During the time of Isaiah's prophecy, which can be read in the
book of Isaiah, chapter forty-five, he foretold that God would anoint
a Gentile king to allow Jerusalem to be rebuilt for the exiles to return
to their native land. Cyrus was that king, and he was over Assyria and
Babylon, enemies to Judah and Israel. Both of these events occurred,
and Isaiah prophesied them 150 years and two hundred years before
they happened.

God made himself known over and over to the Israelites, through
prophets, historical events, and the Torah (the first five books of
the Jewish Bible). Through Isaiah and other prophets, God tells
his people unequivocally that there is no God apart from him. He
said, "I am the Lord, and there is no other; apart from me there is
no God" (Isa. 45:5). God uses whatever means is necessary for each
of us to know there is no other God to whom we can turn so that
we will cry out to him and know his love for us. He is even in the
darkness where we cry out, and he can show us treasure and riches
there. When we do cry out, he calls us by name, as he called Moses
by name. Moses knew God intimately. God favored him, called him
by name, and treated him as a friend.

The Israelites were God's chosen people, but even so they did
not have the access to God that we have today through Jesus Christ.
Through the shed blood of Jesus on the cross and the indwelling
of God's Holy Spirit when we choose to follow Christ, we have an
intimate relationship with the Father. He sees us as perfect through

the death of his Son, a death that atoned for the sins of the world. He names us friends.

In the struggles and dark times, we call upon God, and he hears us. The richest of blessing occurs when we discover he has been with us all along and knows intimately our dark nights. The Father calls out our name, and he becomes a friend by our side. He is God, and there is no other; we know it in a new way, awestruck at his power and love, and humbled before him. We know we are in the presence of our Lord God Almighty, the One who chooses to call us friends.

THE STRENGTH OF MY RIGHT ARM

Day after day, one list at a time, we keep striving to stay the course of our ambitious lives. After all, isn't it the goal that we set early in our careers? What else do we want other than to make partner, to buy the big new house, to secure the club membership? Or is it to make our families perfect, to change the relationship with our parents, to improve our children's schools and education, to help our brothers and sisters in their life course or addictions, or all of the above? Shouldn't we be doing all we can to make our lives better and assist those around us? The answer is yes, but the question is wrong.

Where do we place our energies? Is it our call or God's? Isn't this a spiritual question? Perhaps we would not be striving at all if it weren't for insistence that we do it all in our own time and by ourselves. But the writer of Hebrews tells us to "throw off everything that hinders and the sin that so easily entangles, and let us run with perseverance the race marked out for us. Let us fix our eyes on Jesus, the author and perfecter of our faith, who for the joy set before him endured the cross, scorning its shame, and sat down at the right hand of the throne of God" (12:1-2). Whose race is it? God marks the race for us, and we must run it with perseverance and with our eyes fixed on Jesus Christ; otherwise, it is our own race we are running and we run it without the strength and encouragement of Christ.

I think about the many times I endured hardship and pain because I wanted to do something in my own strength and in my own timing. My eyes were fixed on me, not Jesus. I left no room for God in the equation. The Israelites thought they had conquered their enemies in their own strength, but they were wrong. "With your hand you drove out the nations and planted our fathers; you crushed the peoples and made our fathers flourish. It was not by their sword that they won the land, nor did their arm bring them victory; it was your right hand, your arm, and the light of your face, for you loved them" (Ps. 44:2-3). The battles were won then with God's right arm, and they are won today by God's right arm through Jesus on the cross, enduring the battle and winning the victory for us in this life.

How much strength do I have in my right arm? Has it gotten me any victory lately? When I run the race by fixing my eyes on Jesus, who endured the cross, scorning its shame, and sat at the right hand of God the Father in heaven, I have already won. Victory is mine in him whose right arm established it for all time and forever.

BEING FULLY KNOWN

> But now, this is what the Lord says—he who created you, O Jacob, he who formed you, O Israel: "Fear not, for I have redeemed you; I have summoned you by name; you are mine. When you pass through the waters, I will be with you; and when you pass through the rivers, they will not sweep over you. When you walk through the

fire, you will not be burned; the flames will not set you ablaze. For I am the Lord your God, the Holy One of Israel, your Savior; I give Egypt for your ransom, Cush and Seba in your stead. Since you are precious and honored in my sight, and because I love you, I will give people in exchange for you, nations in exchange for your life. Do not be afraid, for I am with you; I will bring your children from the east and gather you from the west. I will say to the north, 'Give them up!' and to the south, 'Do not hold them back.' Bring my sons from afar and my daughters from the ends of the earth—everyone who is called by my name, whom I created for my glory, whom I formed and made" (Isa. 43:1-7).

When someone accuses you, or dismisses you as insignificant, or describes who you are and misses the mark terribly, it is extremely hurtful. Not to be "known" is most painful when it is by someone who is important to you. Desiring to be understood and loved fully are equal parts of what make us uniquely created by a loving God who wants us to love him and know him fully, as we are fully known by him.

Sometimes we don't want to be "found" (or found out). We prefer not being fully known because we are hiding from everyone, including ourselves. Even then, however, God knows us when we don't know ourselves. He knows every hair on our head, every thought in our head, and every dream or care we may have. We are loved fully and are fully known by him. But sometimes, even in hiding, we do want to be "known." We put on masks or perform so we stand out in some way …even if mysterious or eccentric. During these times we want to be noticed, to feel significant, to be accepted as someone of value, whether we are being real or not.

Knowing and loving are the means by which we will be known.

Loving from a fullness of being loved by God is a daily discipline. It requires that we keep our hearts open to God's presence and his Word. He is the only One who can give us real significance. I don't believe we can give love continually without being filled up from the source, Jesus Christ. With knowing and loving we must first be filled with Christ each day. It is essential to our being to be known. Sometimes when we are wounded we seek the understanding of another. When this is the case, the understanding we seek must be from God, for we cannot receive what we need from others. Our hearts need to be healed by Christ first. When we seek the understanding of another who has wholeness in Christ, we are actually receiving our significance from Christ himself. As we are grow and mature in Christ, we can love, know, and understand *first* with the knowledge that Christ loves, knows, and understands us fully from the inside out.

EXPRESSING FREEDOM—KNOWN BY OUR CALLING

The composer Johann Sebastian Bach said that "All music is for the glory of God." He knew what he composed and shared with the world was from God and for God and by God. When we are doing what our hearts call us to do, we are expressing what God is through us. We are calling out the thing the Creator made us to do. We feel purposeful and significant and known by one greater than ourselves, because without him we would not be able to do this thing he has put in us to do. He is greater than we are and we are his. We must do this thing for God because he calls us to do it. When we are fitted with a purpose, we share in its meaning, even though meaning does not come from it but from God. Yet God gave it to us and we derive pleasure from its purpose, God's purpose.

Expressing Freedom—Known by Our Story

"You have not handed me over to the enemy but have set my feet in a spacious place" (Ps. 31:8) is my story, the story of a mother who desperately prays and finds freedom for her family and her children. She feels compelled to leave what they have known and loved. Then God draws her out into the unfamiliar to bring her to himself in a place where they can be free to be who he created them to be. Each member of this family feels "known" and especially loved and significant because the "spacious place" is uniquely designed for each of them. The story of their lives unfolds to reveal to each of them a gracious, loving, omnipotent God who cares for the smallest details of their days.

Expressing Freedom—Known from the Inside Out in our Creativity

Eric Liddell, the Olympic runner about whom the movie *Chariots of Fire* was made, said that he felt he was created to run. Liddell felt God speaking to him when he ran. There are many ways God speaks to us, including through our physical and mental creativity. Through an imagination dipped in the ink of the Holy Spirit God uses us to call out to all humankind.

Being Known—its Impact

The smallest step, a tiny mustard seed of belief, is all we must make. If we hear God's call in us, we can choose to hear what he has to say. We can live by his direction, taking the instruction of his call and abiding by it, from the inside out. If we determine to live and believe God at his Word, we will make a journey like no other. He promises that "No eye has seen, no ear has heard, no mind has conceived what God has prepared for those who love him" (1 Cor. 2:9). What an impact on our faith will this be! His story will just keep growing in our lives, and this will mean that increasingly we will want to make known what we know to be true, his love and faithfulness to his children, now and forever.

TRAIN UP A CHILD IN THE WAY THAT HE SHOULD GO

It is important for parents to build upon the concept that each of God's children is born with a unique purpose and plan. The job of parents is to guide children in finding and pursuing God's unique purpose for their lives. When our children are taught that God fully knows and loves them, and that they are significant to the Maker of heaven and earth, it will be an important part of their spiritual development.

GOD IS NOT MISSING—-BEING KNOWN

Even if no one in our life knows us for who we are, we are fully known and loved. God is not missing. He knew us before we were born and our days were numbered before he created us in our mother's womb. This is what his Word says in Psalms: "From birth I have relied on you; you brought me forth from my mother's womb. I will ever praise you" (71:6). And, "For you created my inmost being; you knit me together in my mother's womb" (139:13).

Then why are there days when we feel very alone? That may be because we are not at home. God says that as believers we will not feel at home on this earth because our actual home is in heaven. He also tells us that when we believe in him we will have eternity in our hearts, and that the Holy Spirit indwells us. With the presence of the Holy Spirit in our hearts, the truth is we are not alone. God is always with us. We can talk to him about the things that make us feel empty or misunderstood or unappreciated. We can call out to him for solace, and when we do the Bible says God answers before we call. In fact, he knows our very words before we speak them. The Holy Spirit interprets our deep groanings when we have no words and makes intercession for us with the Father (Rom. 8:26). So that we are never alone we can communicate with him, our Creator, our Abba Father, our guide, counselor, and hope.

There have been times in my life when God seems to have been silent, and maybe he was, but I know that he heard me. He may have been telling me to wait before having his answer. I remember events as they happened shortly after one period of seeming silence that were unexplainable and miraculous. God was working and answering me all along. My faith grew more than any other period in my life. The most important thing I learned about this time and others is that I had to continue exercising belief—even though I did not feel the connection to God that I usually did. Feeling alone is a mere feeling and not a fact, for the truth is that God does not go missing and he never abandons or forsakes us.

At other times in my life a turn of events made things more perfect than I could have ever dreamed. A surprise gift or change of plans gave me more than I thought I wanted or expected. God works like this more than we know. He is the one who brings about these serendipitous surprises and show us he knows us better than we know ourselves. He is the giver of all good things. By being grateful, by showing him we notice, by giving him the glory for what he has done, we get to know him better.

BEING KNOWN FOR HOW GOD LOVES US, NOT BY HOW WE LOVE GOD

Just as God wants to be known by how he loves us, more

than anything I want my husband and children to know I have loved them unconditionally and with compassion and truth. How we love God back will never be the real story, but he does make something miraculous out of our believing that he loves us. He loves us unconditionally, perfectly, justly, and compassionately. The truth is that we do not deserve this love, but he gives it unreservedly and faithfully.

If someone ever says, "God loves me because I am good," they are either lying or deceived. God loves us because he does, and that is about all we can say. He is God, and his love is a sheer gift, not something we deserve. A parent who needs a child's love and admiration to feel valued and significant, instead of getting his or her own significance from God, believes the falsehood that they are known by the love that their children have for them. If my children love me, I *must* be valuable. If my children love me, I will not be abandoned. If my children love me, I don't need anyone else. If my children love me, the world can see that I am good and that I have good children. This kind of thinking can be a form of control; the parent needs the child's love so much that they order it so. Sometimes children are left feeling they need to do something for the parent in order to be loved back. The parent's love seems to be conditional, controlling, and sometimes dismissive. In the extreme, when the parent does not get the love that he or she feels they deserve, they can turn the love on and off, or be dismissive or abusive. Out of fear that they are not loved, a wounded parent can continue the cycle of lies, that God's child is not significant, that God's child is not loved, that God's child is not known.

This lie can be the stronghold that keeps families bound for generations. The truth is that God is love and fear has no place. God loves us in spite of what he knows about us. He loves us fully and we are fully known by him. Whether we are parents or children, we are God's workmanship, and we are known and loved fully and unconditionally. We have been purchased by the shed blood of Jesus Christ, who lived and died and rose again so we would have life and freedom eternally.

Joy, Peace, Satisfaction

It is only by being known that we find the joy, peace, and satisfaction for which we are searching in life. For example, we might enjoy telling others of our accomplishments, but the list grows old after a while and we need to do more in our own estimation. Let's say we feel a sense of pride and satisfaction when we finish getting our children through school and into their first jobs. This, however, can be fleeting as well; there will be hard times for our children and sustaining jobs or relationships may bring difficulties for them one day. There is real joy when a son or daughter brings home their first-born, our first grandchild. It is true that grandchildren are tremendous gifts, but even grandchildren are temporary fixes for the God-shaped chasm in our lives. We were made for relationship with God, and only through an ongoing personal walk with Jesus Christ will we find joy, peace, and satisfaction. We are fully known and loved by the Ancient of Days, and through this relationship we have joy, peace, and satisfaction. We can trust him to provide for us, to love us, to know us, to teach us, to hear us, and to lead us through the difficult (and the good) times.

To be in communication with him, God desires our prayers. Does this mean God needs our prayers? The Almighty God of the universe is sufficient without anything from us, including our prayers. Still, he wants us to pray because in prayer he answers our questions and reveals his will. In the process, we know who he is, what he does, and how much he loves us. I have come to know him and how much he loves me through listening prayer and interceding for his Kingdom, my family, and friends.

What a loving God to allow us to participate in his work with his people, to teach us, to grow our faith, to reveal himself to us, and to guide us in ways that grow his Kingdom on earth—which we will not fully know until heaven or until Jesus comes and reigns forever. God knows what we need before we do, and sometimes he answers even before we ask. He creates in us the need for him and his glory, and then he equips us to bring that glory to him.

Another way God communicates with us is by our reading and studying his Word. The Ancient of Days reveals himself through Scripture, and he wants us to know not only what he has done in human history for his people, but also to guide us in our own personal lives. As we come to know the Author of Scripture, he changes our hearts and transforms us into the people he created us to be. The more we gaze into his face through the pages of the Bible, the more he makes us like himself. When we read and study the Word of God, the focus is on understanding, believing, trusting, and serving the God of divine revelation.

Prayer and Scripture are not the only ways God communicates with us. Worship is also an important avenue for coming to know God. In worship believers are united to bring praise to God and to remember who he is and what he has done for us. In worship we corporately confess who we are and how we have gone astray. In worship we acknowledge who and what we believe. In worship we commit to change. God reveals himself to us not only through corporate worship but also through personal worship. He says that wherever two or three are gathered in his name, he is there (Matt. 18:20). God wants us to come together to worship him and to intercede for his Kingdom. We know him better through hearing, listening, and participating with other Christians who know and love the Lord.

In worship the Spirit brings together the body of Christ to accomplish the things he has set forth to do in the kingdom of God. We are his hands and feet in this world, and he equips us to do great things to bring him glory—even things greater than Jesus did, as the Lord himself has said: "I tell you the truth, anyone who has faith in me will do what I have been doing. He will do even greater things than these, because I am going to the Father" (John 14:12). God uses his glory in each of us and in the church collectively for the world to see who he is. Even though we may not know him completely yet, the things we are allowed to accomplish for his Kingdom have eternal significance.

THE PARADOX OF KNOWING AND BEING KNOWN

God loves us, warts and all. He draws us into knowing him, and the more we know him, the more we love him. If we do not come to God and mature in him, we will not know him or love him, and we will not have the completeness or fullness that he has planned for us. In knowing the God of creation we get glimpses of his holiness and perfection, in which he allows us to partake. By faith God grows our knowledge of him and his will on a daily basis. He grows us with the anticipation of our one day knowing him completely and loving him deeply. Just as the Father knows us fully and completely, this same desire has been built into us to be with him and reciprocate his love for eternity.

The grandeur of God, the hope of eternity, the promise of healing, the peace and rest of heaven, the fellowship and celebration of Jesus Christ, the bringing together of all the saints: These are some of the things the Bible tells us we will have in heaven. But eternity does not wait until we are finished with this life. Eternity begins when we decide that we love God, and that Jesus Christ is the Lord of our lives. We can live in this world with things being less than heavenly because we know of the world to come. We were made for the next world. What we need to flourish now is to know, love, and surrender our lives to the heavenly Father by accepting his Son as Savior. When we do that, there is in fact a bit of heaven in this world. God shows us his majesty in the sunset, or in a baby's birth. He tells us we will live with him for eternity. He heals us of our diseases on this side of life or the other side. He gives us peace and rest for our souls when he abides in us with the Holy Spirit at all times. Through his church, which is the body of Christ, we have community and fellowship with other believers and Jesus the Lord. All of these promises and many others are for us because God knows what we need before we do. And with each of these things more and more is revealed about who God is and how much he loves us. The Ancient of Days is a rock and a fortress who allows us to know him and brings us to love him. He lives in us so we can live in hope of loving him fully, just as he has loved us.

Moving the Mountain (It was I)

Have you ever fought so hard to make something work but it stayed the same, or even got worse? Or have you given a dream your all but discovered this was not enough? Going through trials seems like this. So does parenting at times. It is like a long uphill battle with no end in sight. I believe in work and persistence—in not giving up, and this is a good quality if aimed in the right direction. But when perseverance is the end and not the means to an end, then we must examine our course.

Perseverance is something I value and "pride" myself in (first clue). The roles of wife and mother are honorable and worth the hard and sometimes "thankless" work. The daily routine can be boring, and the list of jobs somehow menial and mindless, and even "pointless." When you cook a great meal (you think) and it either isn't eaten or it is eaten in all of five minutes with no conversation (except when someone asks if you know what time the Boy Scout meeting starts), there is room for questioning how meaningful learning to cook is. Yet really appreciating the time at home to work on family living is a huge blessing to me most of the time. On the other hand, I can make it a bigger chore than is healthy for me or anyone else. Let me give a little illustration.

I know that today is a big day for my husband …he has a huge client presentation. My daughter has a college application due tomorrow, and my son has a Scout meeting this evening. After doing all the things on my calendar for the day, I prepare a nice dinner and get myself ready for what may be a really long evening. It will be a long evening for me because I am a morning person, and by five in the afternoon I feel "done" for the day. The other family members are not morning people. My children come in from school and immediately go on to their homework. They take this seriously and I am there if they need me for emotional support and otherwise. My husband comes in from his client meeting, and after greeting one another, he goes on to work some more in his home office. Then the meal is ready and the troops are called. We sit down to eat—and within a couple of minutes we are on to the next thing. More time in the home office for my husband. A meeting for my son. More college applications and homework for my daughter. No conversation, no interaction. For me, it is laundry and making lunches for tomorrow, writing checks for school activities, and making a list of things to do for the next day. By this time I am spent, only to go to bed to wake up and start again. In other words, what I mostly do is persevere.

Of course I *should* persevere in being a wife and mother. It is not that I am climbing the mountain; it is the mountain I am climbing that is the issue. Each day I have a choice to serve God or myself. But often I get in the habit of marking things off of the list, including being available for the members of my family. They need me and I need them, but my heart needs to wait for the timing. My heart desires fellowship with them and that is always good since God made us to have relationships. Persevering in doing the list is self-serving. Giving of our time for the purpose of serving another is godly.

Working in a routine is best for me. Going about a regular daily course is the thing that keeps me going, or the peace that governs my day. God loves order; just look at his creation. He is the Creator and we are to imitate him for our order and our peace. So often the mountain I am climbing is "I," and when that is true I am the obstacle to the journey the Lord has for me. The self-centered person who wants to do things in a certain way to meet a certain destination is not giving God his rightful place in her heart and life, even if she is diligent at being a wife and mother and persevering to make things right as she sees it. I need to surrender the mountain to God (I am the mountain) and let God change my heart into one of service instead of routine and order. He can change my perseverance in climbing over myself into running the race for his sake. The Almighty's race for my family and for me is definitely worth the journey, the work, and the perseverance.

How can we know our work is God's work? We know when we surrender our will as we tell God we desire to live for him instead of ourselves. What do we do when we are working, and nothing seems to be working? The answer is "cry out" to the only One who truly understands and who can truly answer us. He will move the mountain to move on in the journey he has uniquely designed for us—even if we are the mountain. God is the answer to moving the mountain.

A NEW NAME

From the earliest time I can remember, I was cooking for the family, cleaning the house, and taking care of my younger siblings. Made to feel insignificant by those who said they loved me, I suffered depression and loneliness. For many years I chose to control interactions by trying to please them because, more than anything, I wanted their love so that I could love myself. I kept choosing them and their ways, which was death to me, when God wanted me to choose him, which would be life. Instead of trying to manage them, God wanted me to trust him with them. Instead of stepping out in faith and accepting the unfamiliar, I kept doing what was familiar and difficult.

God uses all things to bring us into closer fellowship if we choose to let go of the other things that keep us away. Years of criticism, verbal abuse, and the lies I believed left me with the terrible byproducts of self-doubt and diminishment. Yet God wooed me again to his side, and this time I chose to cling there. I wanted life for me and for my children, and that is what I chose. "This day I call heaven and earth as witnesses against you that I have set before you life and death, blessings and curses. Now choose life, so that you and your children may live and that you may love the Lord your God, listen to his voice, and hold fast to him. For the Lord is your life, and he will give you many years in the land he swore to give to your fathers, Abraham, Isaac and Jacob" (Deut. 30:19-20). I wanted to love the Lord, listen to his voice, and hold fast to the faith, so I started to study his Word. From Scripture I found life-giving words, God's promises, and the truth of the gospel. It is only when we know Truth that we can recognize the world's lies.

Wanting to protect my children from hurt, I used to limit holidays with my family of origin. God, however, used holiday times to show me that he is the protector, not me. One incident on Christmas was abrupt, abrasive, and intentionally hurtful. My children were bewildered and concerned for me, and each separately took me aside to ask privately if I was all right. They all confided they knew my family's ire was directed primarily at me but that it was not really about me. As they got a glimpse of one of many seemingly small but not insignificant betrayals, God let the incident occur in such a way to reveal the perpetrator's hand. My children were surprised by the cruelty, but not hurt by it. It was a familiar yet direct dismissal of me as significant. They saw that this baffled me, but that I was not devastated by the attack. God provided a shield of love around us, and we left the Christmas visit more bonded to each other by divine love and protection.

The prophet Isaiah wrote, "I will give you the treasures of darkness, riches stored in secret places, so that you may know that I am the Lord, the God of Israel, who summons you by name" (45:3). God is so good and yet mysterious in his ways; he shields and defends and confides and thrills us all at the same time. An amazing thing happened later as I was journaling the events of the holiday visit. I was taking hold of something significant God had done in my life. As my fingers pressed the keys, I was about to receive it in full: "What is my new name?" These words appeared on my computer screen. In my heart I knew I was no longer diminished, as my family had intended, but what was this? Then additional letters formed: "My new name is ..." I didn't know where these words came from or what would appear next. But through my fingers God showed me: "My new name is Victor." Victor. A winner. One who defeats the enemy. The words jumped off the screen. As tears flowed down my face, joy bubbled up in my heart, mind, and soul. In this intimate and humbling, awe-filled and holy moment, God's love, approval, and power flowed through me. God, magnificently present, made me accept I was no longer a victim of diminishment by those whose approval I most desperately wanted years ago. Now I am a victor in Christ, whose love, approval, and power I already had.

"Back on the Road"

Turn me around

Turn me back

Take me wherever You are

This day, this hour

Where my hope is

In Your presence with Your guidance

In today on the road

Toward Your purpose, Your life in me

Show me Your hand and heart

As I come to You to embark

On the greatest journey I will have

Because You lead me and strengthen me

I will go wherever You lead

Hold tight to Your truth

Staying close to Your heart

Allow me this hour Your grace

As I falter and misstep

My God picks me up and carries me

And if I'm too weary

Equipping me for what He has in mind

With His strong arms around me

I will stand aright again

He leads me day to day

On the road toward life anew

Back on the road with Him as Guide

To persevere until heaven I awake

Never to journey without sight again

With eyes I will see Him face to face

TRUST

Do not let your hearts be troubled. Trust in God; trust also in me (John 14:1).

Trust in the Lord with all your heart and lean not on your own understanding; in all your ways acknowledge him, and he will make your paths straight (Prov. 3:5-6).

Expect God

Sometimes we already have what we are waiting for, but we have just not received it yet. It is there for the taking, but we have not reached out to take it. God is holding on to us, but we have not taken hold of him. Yet we can ask for and receive what we have in him.

When we ask for God to be with us, we can expect him to be there: "The Lord your God goes with you; he will never leave you nor forsake you" (Deut. 31:6). When we ask God to show himself to us, we can expect he will be with us: "I will lead the blind by ways they have not known, along unfamiliar paths I will guide them; I will turn the darkness into light before them and make the rough places smooth. These are the things I will do; I will not forsake them" (Isa. 42:16). When we ask God for his Word, we can expect he will give it to us: "This is the covenant I will make with the house of Israel after that time, declares the Lord. I will put my laws in their minds and write them on their hearts. I will be their God, and they will be my people" (Heb. 8:10).

When we ask for forgiveness, we can expect to be forgiven: "Blessed are they whose transgressions are forgiven, whose sins are covered. Blessed is the man whose sin the Lord will never count against him" (Rom. 4:7-8). When we ask for God's love, we can expect it: "Give thanks to the Lord, for he is good. *His love endures forever.* Give thanks to the God of gods. *His love endures forever.* Give thanks to the Lord of lords: *His love endures forever*" (Ps. 136:1-3). And when we ask for hope, God does not disappoint: "And hope does not disappoint us, because God has poured out his love into our hearts by the Holy Spirit, whom he has given us" (Rom. 5:5), and "We have this hope as an anchor for the soul, firm and secure" (Heb. 6:19).

What if we were to receive all that we ask and wait expectantly to see the Lord in our lives? Is he too close for us to see him? Has he been carrying us all along? We just have to return the reach of his hand, for his hand is already there waiting for us to take hold. The strong arm of Christ reaches to us from heaven where he sits at the right hand of God the Father. "Exalted to the right hand of God, he has received from the Father the promised Holy Spirit and has poured out what you now see and hear" (Acts 2:33). What an image to keep on the forefront of our mind's eye.

Waiting and Wrestling

We wait on God, not on an event or a person or anything else. If we wait on God, the Lord will renew our strength. Anything else will deplete it.

> But those who hope in the Lord will renew their strength.
> They will soar on wings like eagles; they will run and not
> grow weary, they will walk and not be faint. (Isa. 40:31).

When we are awakened to hear the Lord and to be taught, we have his presence, his insight and instruction, and his Word for others. We long for his awakening in his presence, for that is what completes us.

> The Sovereign Lord has given me an instructed tongue, to know the word that sustains the weary. He wakens me morning by morning, wakens my ear to listen like one being taught (Isa. 50:4).

When we hear him and then see him, we recognize who we are and what we are made of. But until then, we cannot see him.

My ears had heard of you, but now my eyes have seen you. Therefore I despise myself and repent in dust and ashes (Job 42:5-6).

Wrestling it through to the Blessing

In Genesis 32:2-32, Jacob wrestled with God until God blessed him. Jacob became Israel, "because you have struggled with God and with men and have overcome." He named the place "Peniel," "because I saw God face to face, and yet my life was spared." The blessing for Jacob was seeing God, and he wrestled it through to the blessing.

What we do while waiting? Here is an acrostic:

Worship and wrestle for righteousness.

Acknowledge who God is and how we need him.

Intercede for ourselves and others.

Thanksgiving for God's goodness.

Increase in prayer and faith.

Never forget that God is doing a new thing

Give gratitude to the Lord for turning our wailing into dancing.

GOD'S GIFTS IN THE WAITING

We want answers, and we want them now. But God teaches us in waiting that we belong to him and he is in charge of all things. When we relinquish the very thing that keeps us from our knowing that he alone is enough, he gives us the knowing and the love of his presence in the situation. Sometimes we wait a long time to know this because we can't give it up. But sometimes we wait a long time because God has the appointed time in his hands and it is not time. We worship with the knowledge in our hearts that God alone is our all.

"Yet the Lord longs to be gracious to you; he rises to show you compassion. For the Lord is a God of justice. Blessed are all who wait for him!" (Isa. 30:18). Isaiah 50:4, Psalm 27:13-14, Psalm 37:34, Psalm 38:15 and Psalm 130 tell us what the Lord gives us when we wait on him:

- He gives us time to tune in.
- He gives us an awakened heart so we will not miss what he is saying to us.
- He gives us a new kind of active listening.
- He gives us an open heart to receive.
- He gives us a receiving heart to what is offered.
- He gives us the love and strength to open the gift when offered.
- He gives us forgiveness and a forgiving heart.

Therefore, wait wholeheartedly on the Lord.

We desire completion, and God is the only One who can make us complete. He places this chasm in us, a longing for fulfillment, so that we are drawn to him. What do we do in the waiting times? We tune in to God's wavelength, listen with an open heart and mind, and hope for his appointed time. We don't wait on the event or the thing that we want, but rather we wait and hope that God will show himself to us. "Whoever has my commands and keeps them is the one who loves me. And he will show himself, if we are his children: "The one who loves me will be loved by my Father, and I too will love them and show myself to them" (John 14:21).

God gives us his presence and his rest, and he goes where we go to witness to the world that we are his people. When I look at the promises God gave to Moses and how Moses asked for God's favor and blessing on the work he was to do, I am expectant about the work heaven has planned for us (Deut. 33:12-23). God allows us to see his hand in our lives, gives us shelter and protection, and through the death and resurrection of his only Son Jesus he gives us life itself.

The Lord gives us many gifts as we patiently await his full plan unveiled in our lives. Until then, we must observe, watch for, and expect the hand of God on our lives. For most of us, there have been times when we were afraid, or lonely, or could not find our way. And during those times, didn't someone appear? Didn't we receive a call? And weren't we able to rest? God is here now. We can call out to him and wait for his answer. He loves us with an everlasting love, one that favors his children, shelters us, and gives us rest.

"Waiting"

I'm waiting, Lord
For the reach of your hand
For you to strike with force
My shadows lurking demand
I'm waiting for you, Lord
From way down deep
Wrestling, wanting more
My soul, firm secure keep
I hear you, Lord, and wait
Until the doubting ceases
Perhaps the cause abates
Your promises sure to keep
Lord, I'm waiting 'til I see you
Arms around me already been
With eyes raised anew
Face fall down, behold the view
Gifts unopened, already to take
Receiving, expecting His hand
Ask, have, reach, awake
His hope on which to stand
Receive the long awaited
Take the love in, grasp His hand
Forsake the fear, hope to take
On His anchor, I will stand

Daily Track Hope

At the beginning of the New Year, I was praying for my son that he would have hope not in the things or events in his life but that he would have real hope daily. God prompted me to start a calendar on which he could track what he encountered on a daily basis. The idea was for my son to look for ways he experienced hope. Perhaps a person was kind, or a letter came from a friend, or he remembered a Scripture that applies well to a situation at hand. If on a particular day there was absolutely nothing of value to record on the calendar, then he would write a truth about God, such as God is faithful, God will never leave me, or God's love endures forever. The idea behind the calendar is a simple one, but it offers a meaningful way to see God's hand in the seemingly mundane days of our lives. I began using the same calendar, and it has been very effective for me to see God's hand in so many ways I would not have otherwise seen. God's gift of insight always amazes me. He is faithful in drawing us to him in ways we cannot fathom. Whether we grasp his hand or not, he is holding onto us tightly.

Tracking hope this way on a daily basis has been especially helpful with my writing efforts. God's hand and reach are in view more since I am looking for God all day long. What a small way to make ourselves more available for what the Master has in store for us! It is absolutely crucial that we understand that whether we feel the divine nudge or not on a daily basis, he is with us. As we read in the pages of the prophet Jeremiah, "You will seek me and find me when you seek me with all your heart" (Jer. 29:13). We may not always see or experience God, but we can see evidence of him. We can expect him because he is present. God is constantly searching our minds and hearts: "For the eyes of the Lord range throughout the earth to strengthen those whose hearts are fully committed to him" (2 Chron. 16:9). He is always drawing his children to him. We can count on it.

Living without hope is tantamount to trivializing God. Here is why. God is holy, separated from sinful humanity, and yet he comes to us in Christ. In limiting hope we are downplaying God and what he has done for us in Christ. He is the author of all that is truth, love, and mercy. All other facsimiles of him, and especially the ones we create ourselves, will let us down. As the apostle Paul wrote, "Hope does not put us to shame, because God's love has been poured out into our hearts through the Holy Spirit, who has been given to us" (Rom. 5:5).

When we record what we experience on a daily basis, we will see God's hand and heart in our lives. Expect God. He shows up whether we do or not. I have found when I listen to God, really open my heart to him and his Word, I am able to gain learning, insight, serenity, truth, encouragement, and newness.

L   Learning
I   Insight
S   Serenity
T   Truth
E   Encouragement
N   Newness

The prophet Isaiah sums it up when urging us to forget the past (even what is discouraging us at the moment) and expect God and what he has for us. "Forget the former things; do not dwell on the past. See, I am doing a new thing! Now it springs up; do you not perceive it? I am making a way in the wilderness and streams in the wasteland (Isa. 43:18-19). In addition, if we are discouraged by our sin and our past mistakes, Isaiah goes on to say that God will remember our sins no more: "I, even I, am he who blots out your transgressions, for my own sake, and remembers your sins no more" (Isa. 43:25). If we are hopeless and find it difficult to come to God because of our sin, we can come anyway and expect him to do a new thing.

I have learned to expect God at any time, especially when I am walking in his creation. The air seems to stir by his hand, and he makes me see. He makes his presence known in many ways. One way is by his Word written on my heart. It cries out to me to hear it and know it, and in hearing and knowing it his truth becomes real. His grace is evident in my hearing him and knowing him, and his forgiveness is warm and true. At the same time, I notice things inside of me, like the ability to cry out to God, the desire to intercede and plead on behalf of others, the need to wrestle for more and complete righteousness (knowing that he has given it in his Son already), and an overwhelming sense of trust, belief, and gratitude for his grace. He becomes the focus; I am basking in his glory.

In the times of listening and waiting upon the Lord, he comes to us, and in his presence we find mercy, truth, hope, and perseverance. We may not always want to continue on the road, but when we do we know we will not do it alone. At the same time, if the focus becomes the difficult journey, then we will miss the Lord. If we allow our focus to switch to expecting God, we will find that he reveals his hand—and then who knows what will follow …new things … springing up …do you not see them?

LOOKING BACK WITH FORESIGHT

> Then Moses said, "Now show me your glory." And the Lord said, "I will cause all my goodness to pass in front of you, and I will proclaim my name, the Lord, in your presence. I will have mercy on whom I will have

mercy, and I will have compassion on whom I will have compassion. But," he said, "you cannot see my face, for no one may see me and live." Then the Lord said, "There is a place near me where you may stand on a rock. When my glory passes by, I will put you in a cleft in the rock and cover you with my hand until I have passed by. Then I will remove my hand and you will see my back; but my face must not be seen" (Exod. 33:18-23).

As a child of God it is sometimes easy to forget God's tremendous faithfulness to us and recall all he has done on our behalf. As we journey day-to-day we have to remind ourselves—in the difficult times as well as the good times—what the Lord has done for us in the past, how good he has been, how he guided us, and most of all that he is always present with us no matter what the journey.

It is easier to acknowledge the hand of God when we look back on parts of our lives. But we must practice looking back with foresight: practicing the presence of God and knowing that one day we will be looking back and seeing his hand in even our times of hardship. It is this attitude that keeps us from choosing the easier and more disastrous route. Could our determination be the thing he is building in us to ensure our future choices?

When Moses asked to see God's glory, God knew that it would be too much for him to take in. God let Moses see his back when he passed by, and protected him in the cleft of the rock. But Moses was not allowed to see God's face (his glory), "for no one may see me and live." Perhaps we cannot see God's goodness yet, for if it was too much for Moses, it would surely be too much for us. But what we can do is look back and see God in the moment with us. In fact, God wants us to expect that he is in the moment with us all the time.

We have to recognize that the Lord of glory is with us, and when we do, it is remarkable what he shows us. When we ask God the same question Moses did, "please show me your glory," I believe he honors this request. He honored the request in such a way that was remarkable to Moses, and yet at the same time was just a foretaste of what God would do in the future for the Israelites through the Hebrew prophet to show them who he was and how much he loved them. Practicing the foresight of who God is and what he has already done for us gives him praise and acknowledges the covenant God has established with us. Even when we look back as far as we can at our lives and see what God has accomplished for us, it is only a glimpse of what heaven has planned.

UNVEILING

I have been thinking about "unveilings," such as when a bride removes the veil over her head so that her groom can see her face, or when a piece of artwork is unveiled at an art gallery for aficionados to see for the first time. The mask of the desired treasure is drawn away, and the beauty is revealed. This idea of unveiling is exactly what God does when he shows us his glory in Christ Jesus. Our hearts see what has been covered up for us, and then with breaths drawn and eyes awakened we see what God intended for us all along, the face of the Son of Man and the Son of God himself.

When my heart and eyes are unveiled, I know the Father more dearly and see Truth more clearly day by day. But God's timing requires that we wait sometimes. He unveils our hearts when he desires, not when we think he should. He woos us on an eternal timetable rather than a human schedule. For example, I am praying for God's unveiling to a family member. Her heart is obscured, and she cannot see God. What glory she will see when her heart is awakened to the face of Jesus Christ, God himself? Only the

Lord knows that, and only he knows when that will occur. With unveiled faces we see God and we can approach him directly. There is no longer the necessity to go to the temple as the chosen people of Israel had to do. We no longer have to talk to the priest, who was the only one allowed into the Holy of Holies (the inmost chamber of the temple). Jesus reigns in our hearts, the temple of the Holy Spirit. The earth shook and the veil was torn when Jesus defeated death on the cross. It is with unveiled eyes and hearts that we can see and serve God, who gave us life through the death and resurrection of the living Lord.

Seeing Jesus and being transformed by the Holy Spirit means that not only do we have unveiled faces, but we have faces that reflect his glory. The apostle Paul tells us that "Now we see but a poor reflection as in a mirror; then we shall see face to face. Now I know in part; then I shall know fully, even as I am fully known" (1 Cor. 13:12). When we see Jesus face to face one day, we will recognize him because we will look like him. Talk about unveilings. Moses could not let his face be unveiled when he came back from Mount Sinai because once he had beheld the glory of God he was too radiant for the eyes of Aaron and all the Israelites to see. When Moses asked to see God's glory, God told him, "You cannot see my face, for no one may see me and live." What an amazing thing to be able to one day behold the God of the universe face-to-face. But only God can unveil our hearts and eyes so we can be transformed into his likeness so that others may see. What an incredible act to allow us to be part of his glory and his Kingdom on this side of heaven.

PROVISION FOR THE UNFAMILIAR PATH

God provides light for the path. It may be an unfamiliar path, but God's light is sure and it will guide the way on the darkest of journeys. There is a picture hanging in my living room of a path across grassy farmland. I like pictures to which I can ascribe metaphors. Sometimes the sunlight from the window across the room goes straight to this picture and shines in one great beam of light straight on the path across the farmland. It is as if God speaks to me when this happens, and what he is saying is that he will provide light for the journey I am on that particular day. This is especially rewarding when I have been having a dry time in my life and I am unable to feel his presence. That is when I need God's light for the path the most. Isaiah 42:16 says,

> I will lead the blind by ways they have not known, along unfamiliar paths I will guide them; I will turn the darkness into light before them and make the rough places smooth. These are the things I will do; I will not forsake them.

God is faithful and his Word is true. He guides me even when I am not feeling like being guided, or when I am wrestling with him about a desire I have for my life. He says he will not forsake me and that he will turn my darkness into light and make my rough places smooth (Isa. 42:16). I accept God's promise that he makes provision for the unfamiliar path, and I know he will help me with my unbelief. God has a way of providing a path that does not necessarily look the way we think his provision will look. In the Old Testament, God provided a light directly above his people to show them when to continue the journey to the Promised Land and when to stop and make camp. We want God to provide this light how, where, and when we want it, because this is how we will know for sure that he is leading us on the journey. But that is not the way this works. He tells us in this Isaiah 42:16 Scripture that we (who are blind because we cannot see him) will be led and guided on unknown and unfamiliar paths where he will turn the darkness into light before us and where he will make the rough places smooth for us. Whether we can see him—or even the path we are on—we know he is leading and guiding us. These are the things God will do, and he will not forsake them.

No Going Back

When God leads us to a new place we need to remember that there is no going back. So often, we carry our old ways and start behaving in the same old patterns. But God wants us to flourish in the new and to leave behind the old. When we moved into our new home in another part of the city, we had new neighbors, new schools, new places to work (in our home), and new places to surround us, but we began operating in our previous ways. Where is the grocery store around the corner? Where am I going to buy gasoline at the old price? How can I get from here to there? New things and surroundings take some getting used to. On the other hand, the bus stopped right in front of our house and both children rode to school on a bus for the first time in their lives. I had always driven them to school and gotten enmeshed in traffic each day. In our new place the kids had instant friends in the neighborhood, instead of having to drive to others' homes or to other destinations for school activities. The benefits of our move far outweighed the differences, but we were still focusing on what we missed rather than on what God was now providing. It took us a while to remember that God supplied new things for us to prosper.

When I am around my family of origin I tend to take up the role I played when I still lived at home. Often it was a healthy role, but very often it was not. In this case, too, there is no going back. God wants us to be new in our relationships, and we must be ready to change into the people he wants us to be. As he leads us to new places, he is changing us into new people, better and more mature than who we were. We need to accept the gift.

When I first married, I went home a lot because my mother seemed to need me. As I look back, she was probably going through insecurity, the transition of a firstborn being married and worrying that our relationship was going to change. She wanted the security of knowing things were still going to be the same. I kept going home only to be thrust in the middle of their next weekend excursion. I would drive home on Friday evening only for my father to drive to the beach with my mother. She would want me to go along, even if it meant more driving time for me on that day and the next. I went along with it because I also needed security—the security of being needed and pleasing my mother at the same time. God had given me a new marriage, the soul mate of my desires, and I was still in the role of oldest daughter living to please her mother. I was not ready to change into the woman God wanted me to be.

The role of oldest child defined me for most of my life until the burden became so large that I had to surrender it. Doesn't it often come to this? I had to go through a depression and worry that my husband and children were going to suffer (like they weren't suffering already) if I didn't change. They say you will change when the changing is easier than the circumstances that bring it on. A lot of times we just want to remain in the familiar. This is not trusting God. I had to surrender my unbelief. God had to change my unbelief into belief, and I had to grow in the knowledge that believing God was enough, that he was my all in all.

What roles are we still filling because they are the familiar old ones that give us security? What old roles are keeping us from accepting the "newness" God has given us in Christ? Can we not see the "new thing" that is possible if only we would let go of the old? Stepping out in faith requires us to hold on to God and let go of our balance. When we are looking toward God, we don't have to see the obstacles. They will be there, but we don't have to focus on them. It is like standing at the edge of the swimming pool and wanting to jump in the water. He is there to catch us. Only when we take the plunge do we get to experience faith and the joy of the Father's embrace.

Faith happens when we leave the old and come in to the new. My son stepped out in faith when he walked through the school doors this fall. When he saw that God would lead him during the day, he could rest in the knowledge that each new experience would have God in it. My daughter, who is usually filled with anticipation and excitement at new possibilities, also fears things may not work out the way she expects. Her faith is growing as she reaches out to God for direction, and when the time comes, she will take another step of faith to go further on her own journey. My husband walks in faith each day that as he calls on current and prospective clients God will lead him to people with whom he can work and thus provide for his family.

God has a way with time for us. Christ is the Alpha and the Omega, the beginning and the ending. He is eternal, and has no limitations. He knows our dependence on him requires repetition and practice. We have to move forward in our relationship in order to know him more personally, love him more fully, and become who he wants us to be. We cannot go back in time to change things or relive moments in our lives. This is not to say, however, that God cannot use all things to bring us closer to him, including our past.

There is no going back, and we should not live as though we can. Still, many of us dwell on the past, live in the past, or take attitudes with us about the past that keep us from experiencing in the moment the new things God has for us. If I am consumed with anger toward a person, or have guilt over something I have done, or cannot let go of a loved one who has abandoned me in life or in death, I am living in the past. God wants me to deal with it so I can live with him in the here and now. We all have something from our past that needs fixing, and too many choose to cover it up, deny it, or shield themselves from it in order to live with the pain. I have learned personally that is not the way to do it.

I lived for years in the pain I felt over my father's death. Losing my father was very traumatic, and my family unit shattered when he died. Everything that had been covered up seemed to surface. Old illnesses recurred, old wounds rekindled, and words were said because so-and-so was not taking care of so-and-so. Everyone wanted a protector, and no one had the usual one in the family system. We each had our own pain and our own way of dealing with it, and we wanted the other's acknowledgement and help. As the oldest, I thought I needed to be strong for all the others. But I was not strong, and I was in no position to help anyone.

I could not go back. God wanted me to move forward. It took me many years of struggle to hear God and know most of all that he loved me and was sufficient for me. Now that I had a family of my own, and responsibilities that would affect future generations, the Lord was teaching me, "This is not about you." I had placed an extraordinary amount of trust in family relationships, only to be disappointed. I was in extreme pain. Subsequently, I carried that pain into many other relationships. Only through realizing that I lacked trust in God and only when I asked for his help did I begin experiencing the healing that comes from the Great Physician. After years of asking God to allow my children to know that I loved them, I heard him say they did. It was then I came to know he loved me unconditionally. Thus, the healing began. God moves us forward when we say yes to the journey he has for us.

God has done a work in me that is undeniable, unmistakable, and really remarkable. Freedom has new meaning. I know I am vulnerable to being a pleaser and wanting to feel needed, but now I believe I must love the Lord with all my heart, mind, soul, and strength. When I can manage that, God gives me the wherewithal to love others mightily as well. It is only the love of Christ in me that makes the journey worthwhile. My lack of love for others and being full of myself lead me to bondage, self-centeredness, and despair. But the love God provides is full of hope and promise, and it does not disappoint. A new thing is happening; the old is in the past, and there is no going back. God still works in our lives on the things that need repair, but he has new places for us. It is all in his hands, not ours. We are jars of clay the Holy Spirit molds into vessels to be used by him in this day and for eternity.

"Expect God"

Crying out to God to heal

My attitudes and belief

Oh, change the course

To joy from remorse

I'm waiting, Lord, to hear you

To know the pain gone soon

From unbelief to trust, love

All of me to you above

Self-doubt overwhelms me

In the dark night insecurity

Disappointment again makes

Hope yet not to take

You, Lord, have changed my heart

To love, not fear, to believe, not start

Again to doubt the love and grace

You have for me to win the race

Freedom to live without

Believing the lies, the shout

of those who meant to deceive

But depend on Him and receive

The victory in today and eternity

Hope in the land of the living

For light brilliant and night treasure

Things new, mercies beyond measure

"Faith Is"

Keep moving on one step at a time

Yielding myself and my plans

'til through the mountain I've come and beyond

To greater horizons than I've hoped or dreamed upon

He is the treasure within my reach

He comes to move, rest, and speak

In the darkness, in the deep, He moves

To the place He came to teach

The riches stored of His great love

In the mountains, the valleys, and the deep

Can only be found when we seek Him

First and last and all in between then

Seek not to discover His purpose or His plan

But the long reaches of His hand

He is in all that comes our way

As surely as night becomes the day

FREEDOM

Then you will know the truth, and the truth will set you free (John 8:32).

The Spirit of the Sovereign Lord is on me, because the Lord has anointed me to proclaim good news to the poor. He has sent me to bind up the brokenhearted, to proclaim freedom for the captives and release from darkness for the prisoners, to proclaim the year of the Lord's favor and the day of vengeance of our God, to comfort all who mourn (Isa. 61:1-2).

You have not given me into the hands of the enemy but have set my feet in a spacious place (Ps. 31:8).

Memories and Gratitude

When my daughter was confirmed in our church, we decided to have a celebration a few months later on our summer vacation with family and friends. She had accepted Christ into her life at an earlier time, but we wanted her growing up in the church family, and we wanted her to remember her confirmation as a very significant event in her life. To symbolize her new life in Christ, we arranged for her to walk on the shore of a lake. It was to be a symbolic walk, symbolic of the hope and future God has planned for her. During her walk a family member or friend joined her to give her words of encouragement, a gift, a hug, or whatever—essentially they were saying to her that God loves you and has a great future planned for you. Then someone else walked with her for a while, and so on and on. It was special time that included some very significant persons in her life. It was quite memorable for me, too. We all hoped the encouraging words would be remembered as she proceeds on her journey in life.

WHICH THINGS WE ARE PRONE TO REMEMBER

Most of us remember where we were on September 11, 2001. It was such a horrific event that touched all of our lives. Psychologists call this type of memory and how we retrieve it *episodic memory*, a memory caused by a significant event. Other such episodic memories might be triggered by the death of an important national figure, a family member, or where we were when a tornado hit our community. Some things from the past are more difficult to remember without really digging because they were not accompanied by any out-of-the-ordinary circumstances. These events may need to be retrieved by some sort of cue or reminder.

When I was going through a difficult time with my family of origin, old struggles surfaced and bad thought patterns re-emerged. I was afraid a generational curse would reemerge. I was never sure of my own mother's love for me, and I had tremendous fear that my children would not know that I loved them unconditionally. I was a stay-at-home mom and dedicated my life to being a wife and mother. My prayer life was very real to me, as God was surely part of my daily experience. But I was living with strongholds that were limiting my spiritual life. I prayed over and over that God would break the generational curse in my family and that my children would know his love for them and my love for them as a mother. God is faithful, and he honors prayer. And he surely wanted this for my children as much as he wanted it for me.

On my walk one morning, I asked again for the generational curse to be broken. It was like a light came on and I finally heard God say, "They do know and they will know that you love them." What I know now is that God answered that prayer as he does even before we ask: "Before they call I will answer; while they are still speaking I will hear," says Isaiah 65:24. But I just hadn't received his answer in my heart. I will never forget that walk. The sun was shining. I remember the curve in the road and just how I felt when my heart received God's love for me and for my children. It was truly amazing grace. Sometimes, when the morning light is cast a certain way, or if I am on that curve in the road, I recall the feeling I had as God spoke to my heart that day. These episodic memories or cues are significant in my life journey. Later on that morning walk I picked up a rock on the path to remind me of God's answer. I probably don't need the rock to remind me of his goodness, because since that time I have carried his love every day for my children and me.

Other answers to prayer are also significant and need to be remembered. They may need memory cues associated with them. For example, I have a "thesis dress" I have saved through the years because it reminds me that God brought me through the writing of a master's thesis, and the dress serves to remind me to be grateful to God for all that has transpired and is happening in my life. For me the master's degree was not a clean sweep but a struggle where I learned God provides not in my time frame but his.

Another example is that when I study the book of Jeremiah, it brings back my junior high Sunday school days and the teacher talking about Judah and the southern kingdom. I don't remember much of what she taught us during those lessons, but I do remember she loved us and she loved God's Word and wanted us to love it also. I wanted what she clearly had—a personal relationship with Christ. She was a beautiful elderly woman, full of spunk and wisdom. She didn't have much materially, but she was rich in relationship. She spoke with remarkable strength and loved with her eyes. She was a truly joy-filled person, even though her life might have seemed bleak by the world's view. She lost her husband early in life, and one of her daughters died at a young age. My teacher was poor and alone most of the time, but these were not the things one saw when in her presence. Rather, what one saw was Jesus in her life. I can't read Jeremiah anymore without being reminded of God's love and presence.

"MEMORY MINDING" AND MEMORIAL STONES

"Memory minding" cues us to remember how God provides for and enriches our lives in specific ways. Remember how God told the Israelites to teach their children all they have been taught and not to forget what he had done for them? "Take to heart all the words I have solemnly declared to you this day, so that you may command your children to obey carefully all the words of this law. They are not just idle words for you—they are your life. By them you will live long in the land you are crossing the Jordan to possess" (Deut. 32:46-47).

We go to great lengths to make memories with and for our children. Therefore, shouldn't we desire to enrich their lives with things reminding them of God's provision? How is it even possible we can take for granted the daily provision of our God? We are to teach our children and their children to obey carefully all the words of God's law. We are to "impress them on your children. Talk about them when you sit at home and when you walk along the road, when you lie down and when you get up. Tie them as symbols on your hands and bind them on your foreheads. Write them on the doorframes of your houses and on your gates" (Deut.6:6-9). In other words, we are to tell them the stories of our generation and the generations before.

God has said we can be confident that "he who began a good work in you will carry it on to completion until the day of Christ Jesus" (Phil. 1:6). What this actually means is that the prayers we pray will still be honored after we die …until the Day of the Lord. This is so monumental to me. I am awed that God would listen to us in the first place, but for him to keep blessing the generations after us with our prayers and even the prayers of those before us is mind-boggling. Praying for our children is ministering to them now and for generations afterward.

God says he will bless a thousand generations after us if we keep his commandments: "Know therefore that the Lord your God is God; he is the faithful God, keeping his covenant of love to a thousand generations of those who love him and keep his commands" (Deut. 7:9). What richness of mercy to us and our children and to all the generations before and after us. How can we not tell our children about God's great work in us and around us?

When we teach our children the history of God's dealings with humanity, it will make a difference in our lives and theirs. I have been so drawn to the story of the Israelites crossing the Jordan River. God told them to pick up twelve memorial stones in the river as they passed through it so Joshua could set them up at their camp at Gilgal. The Lord told Joshua to do this so that "In the future when your descendants ask their fathers, 'What do these stones mean?' tell them, 'Israel crossed the Jordan on dry ground.' For the Lord your God dried up the Jordan before you until you had crossed over. The

Lord your God did to the Jordan just what he had done to the Red Sea when he dried it up before us until we had crossed over. He did this so that all the peoples of the earth might know that the hand of the Lord is powerful and so that you might always fear the Lord your God" (Josh. 4:21-24).

What memorial stones do we need to set up? What reminders do we need to call upon so we will always remember that the hand of the Lord is powerful? In computer systems there are retrieval cues to help the computer bring up information stored in memory. In the human mind, this is done through recalling certain events, sights, tastes, smells, sounds, or words. When we want to remember something, how valuable would it be if we could relive the things that God has done for us through the use of memory reminders, such as the memorial stones of the Israelites?

We use our own version of memorial stones when we exchange rings for weddings, cut off locks of hair for births, or paste pictures into photo albums. Why don't more of us use memorials to remember the riches, treasures, provision, and gifts of God? If we did, we would remember to be grateful. We would remember to *remember*. When we are in the valley, we would remember God's mountaintop. When we are sick and lonely, we would remember that God is omnipresent— with us everywhere and always. We would remember that God is with us even in the darkness.

Using memory minding techniques and memorial stones would help us model the behavior that God prescribed for the Israelites. We can recall to our children how God provided for us and we can show them reminders of his blessings in our everyday lives. Then we can ask them how God is active in their lives, or help them remember when God answered a prayer, or when he provided for them in just the perfect way. Teaching our children to be grateful by remembering our God and his current and future provision is a privilege and a necessity. We remember for ourselves and we remember to impress our experiences of God on our children, "so that all the peoples of the earth might know that the hand of the Lord is powerful and so that you might always fear the Lord your God."

Remembering the Ways You have Known God's Provision

Moving across the river to a new home for my family was like crossing the Jordan into Gilgal, where the Israelites put up memorial stones so they wouldn't forget what God had done for them. We went on a family vacation to see the historic sites and monuments in Washington, D.C., during the first spring break after our move to a new home. A few days after we returned, I thought about how good God had been to us through the move, the change of schools, the larger house, the nicer neighborhood, meeting new friends, keeping old friendships, and so on. When I was walking one morning, I kept noticing the big rocks in the yards of many of my neighbors. I remembered the story of the Israelites crossing the Jordan and how we had recently crossed our own Jordan. God had delivered us to a new land, and I thought we needed to remember this as a family. God seemed to say to me that if we used memorial stones "even the rocks will cry out to praise me." I want to praise him with my life and I want to teach my children to be grateful and to praise God every day.

We were having a family devotional time on a Sunday morning after the trip, and we talked about what we had seen and learned, and how God had moved through history providing for our nation. We saw many monuments of God's provision, such as the Washington Monument, the Jefferson Memorial, the Lincoln Memorial, the

DC War Memorial, Arlington National Cemetery, and the U. S. Holocaust Memorial Museum. We decided we needed to have three memorial stones for our journey, which became *truth*, for God is truth, *trust*, because we have to trust him, and *freedom*, for only with God can we be free to be who he has designed us to be. These rocks remind us of divine deliverance of our family to a spacious place, and the freedom to live out his story in our lives.

WHAT MAKES US REMEMBER?

My husband asked this question of the minister who married us: "What gets you through the tough times?" The answer stays in my mind: "I was most fortunate in that I had several people along the way who encouraged me. I remember their voices." Encouragement from others is another form of reminder that God loves us, and often it comes to us in this form. What a wonderful thing to be encouraged by others when the times get tough, when things are not so great. And encouragement goes the other way, too—from us to others. God gives us hearts and minds to choose what we will believe and think, and even what we choose to remember. Some people have had horrific and terrible tragedies in their lives, and God can use us in their lives when they remember our voices used for encouragement.

A decision to recall how and what God has done for us is a choice, one that God asks us to make. He says we are to recall his love, mercy, forgiveness, faithfulness, and sovereignty all day long, and in what has to be one of the shortest verses in the Bible, he tells us to "pray continually" (1 Thess. 5:17). We are to think on the good things, as the apostle Paul has written: "Brothers, whatever is true, whatever is noble, whatever is right, whatever is pure, whatever is lovely, whatever is admirable—if anything is excellent or praiseworthy—think about such things" (Phil. 4:8). We are to be grateful in all things: "Give thanks in all circumstances, for this is God's will for you in Christ Jesus" (1 Thess. 5:18). Deciding to recall God's love, faithfulness, and sovereignty, and deciding to recall things that are lovely and admirable is a daily and, actually, a moment-by-moment decision.

One usually tries to make decisions by choosing the better option in a given situation. When God tells us we can choose either life with his blessings, or death with his cursings, which is the better choice? Deuteronomy 30:19 has it this way: "This day I call heaven and earth as witnesses against you that I have set before you life and death, blessings and curses. Now choose life, so that you and your children may live." I am reminded of this verse often when I dwell on the dark places in my past or do things that are not good for me or those around me. Quickly it corrects my thinking. I have the strength in me through Christ to choose life and God's blessings. God speaks through his Word that he is alive and with us even in the darkest of moments, because he loves us and wants life for us. He said, "I will give you the treasures of darkness, riches stored in secret places, so that you may know that I am the Lord, the God of Israel, who summons you by name" (Isa. 45:3).

My heart and mind have to cooperate with the Holy Spirit in me and *believe*. I may need to be reminded of God's enduring love, in which case his Word will guide me. I can also recall how God has provided in the past for me. These memory minders (memorial stones in my life) become very important to my faith walk. They are also important to my family and those around me as God's testimony in my life.

How does the act of remembering help our outlook? For one thing, we have less fear because we know that God is who he says he is as we practice faith in Christ. The trust we have in the Father

arent in our habits and in our choices. Gratitude becomes

because we are choosing life and God's blessings. His

over our fear and he reminds us more and more who is

in charge. It becomes a cycle of life that is more dynamic in praise and thanksgiving and more conscious of who God is and what God has to do in our lives. We become more like children who want to please him and more trusting of his plan and more thankful that he is our Father and our Sovereign God.

This is the God of Abraham, Isaac, and Jacob. He is the Great I AM. He has a plan for our lives that is rich and purposeful. As we come to know who God is we learn to love him more and live for him more. Let's remember.

A Strategy for Daily Living and Remembering

By design we are habitual people. We are also designed to want to be loved and to show love. We want to be known; we need to be called by name. We take things personally. God wants each of us to know him personally, as he knows each of us, including the number of hairs on our heads, the thoughts in our minds, and the desires of our hearts. In our desire to be known we sometimes seek bad things, things that are unhealthy to seek. It is a good thing to want to be known, for God made us that way. But we can get ourselves into real trouble with the illegitimate and indiscriminate use of the desire to be known.

To encounter the God who wants to be known means learning about him, spending time with him, and reading about who he is, what he has done, and what he is doing in our world. He knows each of us by name, and he does not forget. He has said, "See, I have engraved you on the palms of my hands" (Isa. 49:16). In order to love someone we must choose to do so. That means giving up a part of our own world in order to enter theirs. God asks that we do that to get to know him, and so choosing him requires a decision on our part. Once we choose life in Christ, we then embark on the journey of a lifetime, when we are to remember him in all ways. Proverbs tells us to "Trust in the Lord with all your heart and lean not on your own understanding; in all your ways acknowledge him, and he will make your paths straight" (Prov. 3:5-6).

Since we are habitual we need to be reminded to do the same thing over and over again. And we need to be reminded that God loves us, provides for us, and forgives us. God tells us to listen to him and he will direct our paths and make them straight, ones designed specifically for us (Ps. 25:12). Over and over again we are reminded in Scripture that God is loving, forgiving, and knowing. He knows us inside and out, in all our puniness. When we forget these things, he draws us back through reminding us. When we build up a reservoir of reminders, of how he has provided, shown us the way, gotten us through hard times, called us by name, or given us mercy when we didn't deserve it, we can be drawn back all the more easily. We will see him more clearly because we have seen how he works in our lives and how he is drawing us in. God uses our situations and words to remind us of his lessons. He is right there to remind us that we are his children and that we need his love. And he is there to remind us to pay attention to his ways and his teaching. He calls us by name to love us and guide us on his path. Some of God's guidance might not feel like loving at first, but it is. I have seen his hand like this before.

God wants us to be his image bearers, with hearts like his, thoughts directed heavenward, and lives representative of divine love, truth, and mercy. We cannot do that unless we know him and love him and keep our minds on him. We are to "run with perseverance the race marked out for us. Let us fix our eyes on Jesus, the author and perfecter of our faith, who for the joy set before him endured the cross, scorning its shame, and sat down at the right hand of the throne of God" (Heb. 12:1-2). Jesus will keep reminding us that he loves us, so let us keep remembering our hearts must be full of him, which happens as we choose to remember him and run with him.

THE JOURNEY BEGINS NOW

What if someone has no pleasant memories, milestones, or days to celebrate? What of remembering in that case? What we need to know is that the journey begins now. We are not to dwell in the things of the past but instead know that God is doing something new in our lives (Isa. 43:18-19). The more in tune we are to God's work, the more we notice what he is doing in us and around us. Maybe we have endured too many struggles. Maybe we have had a lifetime of hardship and sorrow, to the point that it is difficult believing God loves us. But today something has touched our heart, and we felt a "pull" to know more. Now we are wondering if God does love us and wants us to have memories and gratitude. I can tell you he does. He loves his children. We are the apple of God's eye, according to Deuteronomy 32:10: "In a desert land he found him, in a barren and howling waste. He shielded him and cared for him; he guarded him as the apple of his eye." He wants to show us he loves us, and the greatest way he has done this is in the life, death, and resurrection of Christ Jesus.

God invites us to know him. He has planned a journey for all people that includes Christ at the center of lives that allow his Word to penetrate their hearts. The more grateful we are for whatever is going on in our lives, the more faith we will have, the more gratitude we will have, and the more we will know the Savior's guidance. He will lead us through the journey with milestones of courage and faith that we never dreamed possible.

Our journey of memories may begin today with the question, "Why would God love me?" The question itself may be the memory cue of the Lord's story in our life. It may begin the journey of God drawing us to him in an unquestionable way. All we need to do is take the step of faith and ask the question. The Holy Spirit of God is waiting for us to open the door of our hearts to him. Jesus said, "Here I am! I stand at the door and knock. If anyone hears my voice and opens the door, I will come in and eat with him, and he with me" (Rev. 3:20). For all the answers one will ever need, open the door and let him in. Every answer will be a reminder of a treasure found in Jesus Christ, and every answer will point to additional riches in him.

Our Story and Our Family Stories

Our faith stories start with an ending because we step out of something old into something new. What is new is faith, though it may be faith as tiny as a mustard seed. Still, that faith can be sown and grown. Jesus said, "I tell you the truth, if you have faith as small as a mustard seed, you can say to this mountain, 'Move from here to there' and it will move. Nothing will be impossible for you" (Matt. 17:20). He also said, "If you have faith as small as a mustard seed, you can say to this mulberry tree, 'Be uprooted and planted in the sea,' and it will obey you" (Luke 17:6). One little step is all we have to make, and God grows us with each one. The story of our lives is not just a beginning that starts with an ending. It is actually the middle of something greater and more encompassing. God is doing something big, and our steps become part of it. This is God's story in our lives, which is part of his story for all time and all eternity. It is amazing to be a part of something as great as God's entire plan for all humankind.

Moses tells the Israelites what God revealed to him on Mount Sinai:

> These commandments that I give you today are to be on
> your hearts. Impress them on your children. Talk about
> them when you sit at home and when you walk along
> the road, when you lie down and when you get up. Tie
> them as symbols on your hands and bind them on your
> foreheads. Write them on the doorframes of your houses
> and on your gates. When the Lord your God brings you
> into the land he swore to your fathers, to Abraham, Isaac
> and Jacob, to give you—a land with large, flourishing
> cities you did not build, houses filled with all kinds of
> good things you did not provide, wells you did not dig,
> and vineyards and olive groves you did not plant—then
> when you eat and are satisfied, be careful that you do not
> forget the Lord, who brought you out of Egypt, out of the
> land of slavery (Deut. 6:6-12).

After the death of Moses, Joshua led the Israelites and reminded
them what God wants them to do:

> On the tenth day of the first month the people went up
> from the Jordan and camped at Gilgal on the eastern
> border of Jericho. And Joshua set up at Gilgal the twelve
> stones they had taken out of the Jordan. He said to the
> Israelites, "In the future when your descendants ask their
> parents, 'What do these stones mean?' tell them, 'Israel
> crossed the Jordan on dry ground.' For the Lord your
> God dried up the Jordan before you until you had crossed
> over. The Lord your God did to the Jordan what he had
> done to the Red Sea when he dried it up before us until
> we had crossed over. He did this so that all the peoples
> of the earth might know that the hand of the Lord is
> powerful and so that you might always fear the Lord your
> God (Josh. 4: 19-24).

The psalmist does what God tells them to do for their children and their children's children:

> My people, hear my teaching; listen to the words of my mouth. I will open my mouth with a parable; I will utter hidden things, things from of old—things we have heard and known, things our ancestors have told us. We will not hide them from their descendants; we will tell the next generation the praiseworthy deeds of the Lord, his power, and the wonders he has done (Ps. 78:1-4).

God reminds us through Moses, Joshua, and the psalmist that he has done great things for which he alone gets the credit. And God tells us to pass the stories of these things on to our children and to their children as a way to remember him and the great things he has done for us. It is also a way to continue being grateful to God and to worship him. It teaches our children the ways of God and who he says and demonstrates he is.

We have our stories of faith to pass on, starting in the middle of a greater story—God's.

BEGINNING WITH AN ENDING

In *Family Faith Stories*, Ann Weems says, "Our faith story begins with an ending." I particularly like this quote because it speaks of newness and of leaving the old behind. I came up with my own version of this quote with a list of endings and beginnings of the faith walk I am trying to live out. God is faithful!

The ending of fear
is going out in faith.

The ending of bondage
is living in freedom.

The ending of *my* knowing
is believing in God knowing.

The ending of my pursuing perfectionism
is knowing God in Christ, who is perfect.

The ending of self-doubt
is believing that God is growing me up in his time.

The ending of me having to work everything out
is trusting in the redemptive and healing work of Christ in my life.

The ending of living in the past and the future
is living in the presence of God throughout the day.

The ending of despair and disappointment
is living in the hope and courage of Christ in me, the hope of glory.

The ending of holding on to past grievances
is beginning to let go, and live in mercy and forgiveness.

The ending of holding on to familiarity and my order of things
is walking in faith where God leads me.

Father God, grant me a listening at a new level, and new ears to hear. And most especially, grant me a grateful and courageous heart to obey. "The Sovereign Lord has given me a well-instructed tongue, to know the word that sustains the weary. He wakens me morning by morning, wakens my ear to listen like one being instructed" (Isa. 50:4).

SHARING GOD'S FAITHFULNESS

Sometimes I have a difficult time sharing what God has done in my life. It is not because I don't want to shout from the mountaintops what is going on with me, but because it might sound too righteous or make me sound holier than thou—like I'm bragging. How could this be? Am I feeling like God favored me because of something I have done? Or is it that God has favored me and I am not used to receiving his favor? I know God blesses me all the time, but I don't always acknowledge it when he does. I want to change. I know in my heart and mind that God's favor is not earned or deserved. When he gives his favor he gives it freely and without conditions, and we are to receive it and let it transform us. This is a new thing to me. God wants us to receive his grace and kindness, and he wants us to let the receiving do a work in us. It is worth thinking about this some more and fleshing it out.

When I receive a compliment, I have learned not to quibble over it. The best thing to do is simply say "thank you." If I don't accept the compliment and let it sink in, I have not really received the gift of the expression. This may be a small thing, but if we miss too many small things we similarly may miss the big things. God's favor or blessing is a huge thing, not to be taken lightly. It must be received in the way he has given it since it is his desire for us to have it. What would it do in our lives if we really let it sink in, if we took it, relished it, lived it, and let it do a work in us?

What does receiving God's favor have to do with sharing God's faithfulness? It has everything to do with it, because when we share something he has given we are owning it, acknowledging that this is God's favor and saying what he is doing in our lives. Perhaps that is what feels a little strange to me. God has given it to me and out of gratitude I want to share it with someone. It makes the gift more real to me and allows God's blessing to work in my life and in another's. Recently I had lunch with a longtime friend who has seen me struggle with issues in my family of origin. I had a tremendous breakthrough. God gave me victory. In sharing God's faithfulness with her today, my story of God's favor became more real to me ... more victory!

Praise God, from Whom all blessings flow;

Praise Him, all creatures here below;

Praise Him above, ye heavenly host;

Praise Father, Son, and Holy Ghost. AMEN.

TRUTH, TRUST, AND FREEDOM

I want my children to believe that "God is good; he is faithful. We remember and we are grateful." The faithfulness of the Almighty is the foundation upon which all else stands. I have had the absolute fortune of a journey where God taught me these things and wants me to pass them on to my children to be remembered for the generations. My story is not unusual in God's economy, but it is uniquely mine to share. Every Christian has a unique story, and that is one more amazing way God works.

As I have already written, a few years ago I felt the divine nudge to look into different schools for my children. What God did was the unexpected, and it taught us that he is sovereign and has every detail of our lives in his hands. I began looking around at other schools in the area, and I asked God for truth as we began the process. The verse that unmistakably kept me going was Psalm 31:8, which reads, –"You have not handed me over to the enemy but have set my feet in a spacious place." I still remember the school open house where this verse came clearly to my mind and heart. I took that as a promise and I prayed about it quite often. We looked high and low and were still not excited about our options. Finally we surrendered our location and prayed for the move that we felt God was guiding us toward.

After living sixteen years in one location, we moved to another part of the city where the public schools were known for their great education. The new home was across the main river in town in a small neighborhood community with a swimming pool right across from our house. Our children were born while we lived in the old home, so needless to say we were attached. But God wanted us to cross the river.

Our journey across the river was certainly not as dramatic as the Jews crossing the Jordan River on dry land into the Promised Land. Yet I believe our journey was just as decisive and valid. The Israelites were instructed to set up memorial stones to remember how God had delivered them as he promised. While I was walking in my new neighborhood, I noticed the rocks on the neighborhood lawns. Was I supposed to set up stones to remember our journey? We decided we needed to remember our journey with three stones to be symbols of Truth, our need to trust God, and the freedom he gave us in a spacious place.

God is so faithful. During our time of looking for just the right stones and where to place them, many more reminders have occurred. Our son became gravely ill in the spring after our move. While he was in the hospital, our minister was traveling in the Holy Land. One day he called and said, "I just had to call you and check on you. I am on my cell phone crossing the Jordan into Jericho." What a blessed reminder that God is in the details!

Our stones are a reminder that we must trust God and that we have freedom through our Lord Jesus Christ. Our children know our story, and they are to tell their children one day. "In the future when your descendants ask their fathers, 'What do these stones mean?' tell them, 'Israel crossed the Jordan on dry ground'" (Josh. 4:21). The stones are a reminder to us and to generations to come that God is good, that he is faithful, and that we must be grateful for what He has done.

You are kind, Our God
Your goodness is astounding
My heart receives
My soul rests
In your unfailing love

You provide, Our God
You withhold no good thing
From those who call upon you
My heart receives
My soul rests
In your unfailing love

You guide me into your truth-all truth
You level the mountains
You light the path
My heart receives
My soul rests
In your unfailing love

You heal, transform, restore, and free me

Your ways are not mine, nor your thoughts

You are God alone; there is no other

My heart receives

My soul rests

In your unfailing love

My heart sings; my soul cries out with praise

How do you love me but you do

Our God loves, forgives, provides, and guides

He heals and frees His children

Everyone who asks, seeks, waits and hopes for Him

My heart receives

My soul rests

In your unfailing love

He only is worthy of praise

Shout, cry out His Name above all names

Lamb and Lion, Mercy and Truth, Our God

I will watch for Him with hope

I will wait for Him

He will hear me and save me

My heart receives

My soul rests

In your unfailing love

REVERSAL OF DESTINY—GOD'S STORY IN MY LIFE

> The secret things belong to the Lord our God, but the
> things revealed belong to us and to our children forever,
> that we may follow all the words of this law. Deut. 29:29

A dictionary definition of *destiny* would be a predetermined course of events often held to be an irresistible power or agency. But *destiny* from an unlovely and unlovable point of view (mine) would be a life not desirable to me. It would be giving up my hopes/desires/dreams for the hopes/desires/dreams of my mother. My life was to make her happy, even though I knew I could not make her happy, and even though whatever she thought would make her happy would definitely spell misery for me. Because I was unlovely and unlovable, I was not significant. To find significance I had to run from my destiny, to be known by my achievements, discipline, and perseverance—such as being at the top of my high school class, winning many piano competitions throughout my school years, being awarded college scholarships, and earning graduate degrees.

I desired more than anything to be loved and affirmed. I wanted this so much it consumed me. If only one family member recognized my achievements, I would be whole. But that did not happen. Actually, it is probably good that did not happen because if I had been approved, I would be living an undesirable life. Why? Because I wanted my mother's love so much that I would have sacrificed my own achievements. In many ways my story is a story of reversals. But God is in the business of destinies, and he has big plans for us, plans that include a future and a hope, in spite of us. He put it this way in the book of the prophet Jeremiah: "'For I know the plans I have for you,' declares the Lord, 'plans to prosper you and not to harm you, plans to give you hope and a future'" (Jer. 29:11).

My mother lives in a place inside of herself and from there she dominates others and everything in order to create an environment where she can thrive. She usually gets her way and has for most of her life; she is a beautiful woman who is smart and amazingly cunning. She laughs a lot and enjoys entertaining people with her antics, even at the expense of others. She loves crossword puzzles and is extremely good at them, and she fills her days with mental activities. Words are my mother's long suit.

Sadly, however, she hurts and manipulates with them. As long as she is on top in a situation, she is the life of the party and comes off as the happiest person alive. She is not one who has learned to empathize and has no interest in caring for anyone else. Because of her desire to dominate, she does not want others close to her. Thus, her life is completely lonely. Nor does she want to address the things she does that hurt other people. "They are too sensitive," she will say, as if she has more substance than they. She shows the most antipathy toward her children.

With her type of mental disorder, my mother could not be there for us, her children. We were her means to an end to get her needs met. While we wanted and needed a mother, what I know now is that she could only be and do what her lack allowed, which was diminishing and harmful to us. Even though my destiny and that of my siblings was to serve my mother in every capacity in her distorted view, God had another plan. But until I took hold of God's plan, my life was under the influence of my mother's state of mind and her spiteful schemes. Her plan was to always have one of her children available close by to tend to her needs, one by one, night or day. Most normal mothers love having their children close by, but they want them to live their own full and satisfying lives. That never entered my mother's mind. No matter what role she had us play, we all bowed to her superior position, realizing whatever we were asked to do would be inferior to anything she did. She was always at the top of the hierarchy, no matter what lie she had to fabricate. These words sound so harsh, even to me, but it is a horrible thing for children to live knowing their mother has malicious intent for them.

Now on the other hand, knowing that a mentally ill mother has a huge void in her life gives perspective and hope for children. Knowing this validates that what occurred in their lifetimes as children happened because of an emotionally distant mother and not because of anything they did themselves.

Destiny Reversal Beginnings

The very thing that scared me the most was having children of my own, and here I was with our first child, our daughter. She was the most beautiful thing I had ever seen, a perfect gift from God. I didn't deserve her. A strange notion kept coming to my mind: What if she never knows how much I love her? What if I can't show her my love in a way she understands? This was my fear when she was a tot. I cried out to God to intervene and have her know I loved her and that he gave me the greatest gift of all. In my own case, I knew from my head to my heart that God loved me. And I knew he loved my daughter in the same way. But would he show her—and would she know—that I loved her? Would God use my search for love for my daughter to help me realize not only his love for me and for her, but my love for her?

The vulnerable times in one's life when betrayal, loss, or disappointment occurs invariably bring to mind other times of pain. Every hurt I incurred took me back to my old childhood pain. I thought I needed what I didn't have, the love of a mother. But God wanted me to know him, to know that he loved me more than any mother ever could, and that he could fill that hole in my life with himself. With each step I took that brought me closer, the Lord helped me peel another layer off. He taught me his truth from his Word and helped me see the lies that diminished me and made me feel like an unloved person. He taught me that I had tried hard enough to make the relationship right with my mother. He taught me to handle disappointment by bringing it to him, and he brought me into his arms to shield and protect me as I turned each hurt and painful memory over to his care. Instead of running to another relationship where I felt safe, at least until I was disappointed, he allowed me to see that I was running after the wrong thing. God taught me that if I didn't know where I was going, then I would take the familiar route and once again end up where I didn't want to go. If I am searching for the thing I cannot have and keep going back, I will end up where I don't want to be in spite of myself. As long as I kept doing things my way, an undesirable destiny loomed in my future, a destiny far inferior to the one God had in mind for me.

I have learned it is not enough to know what you do not want. You have to know what you do want. God stirred up a desire in me to know him. I knew I wanted to be a mother who loved, cared for, and protected her children, including giving them sufficient affirmation. I also wanted them to know that God loved them as his children, and so did I. They are his treasure, people to be highly valued in all ways. I am awed and grateful beyond words that God taught me these things and that he is helping me teach them to my children.

Another thing I have learned is that it is not enough to keep from thinking bad thoughts about yourself and others. The better way is to replace one's own thinking with the teaching of Scripture. God has given me a thirst for his Word, and I live by the Word of God that is written on my heart. The apostle Paul wrote, "You show that you are a letter from Christ, the result of our ministry, written not with ink but with the Spirit of the living God, not on tablets of stone but on tablets of human hearts" (2 Cor. 3:3). His Word is replacing all the negative thoughts and diminishment that I learned as a child. God was there all along, waiting for me to run to him. He fills my God-shaped emptiness with himself and replaces the lies I believed with his Word that describes who he says he is and what he stands ready to do in our lives.

A reversal of destiny is God's story in my life. He has turned me around to look into his face and see the love he has for me, a love that is unfailing, forever with me, and never changing. With the Father's unconditional love I am able to love those around me and trust him with the direction I should go. His plan is for a future and a hope, a destiny that far outweighs what I can ask or imagine.

God has our Destiny on His Heart

Are we turned toward God to see his face? Are we ready for a reversal of destiny? God's story always includes reversals. He can use the worst of things for our good if we let him. My reversal of destiny began with my deliverance from unbelief and the lies and deceit of the Evil One. God reversed my destiny by delivering me from a destination of my own making, then setting me down in a spacious place, and then leading me to the freedom of knowing and receiving his love. My destination is in him, for he is my life, my story, and my song (Deut. 30:19; Ps. 30:11-12; Ps. 31:8).

God creates all reversals of destiny to end in him. That is what redemption is all about. He turns our lives around from destruction, self, and dead-end roads leading nowhere. Until we realize our lives are in Christ, we will not live in freedom. Jesus, who is God incarnate (wrapped in flesh), lived to serve us in obedience to God, our Father, and to speak the message of God's forgiveness of our sin and our freely offered salvation through faith in his Son. Jesus, who was God himself, did not do anything except by God's hand and command. If God tells us he is our life, that we belong on a higher plane, and that he loves us enough to sacrifice his Son on our behalf, we need to believe him and lean completely on him. From what or whom do we need to be rescued? God has not handed us over to the Enemy. No, what he desires for us is to live in a spacious place. Our destiny is freedom.

God wants us to take his outstretched hand and hold it tightly so he can set us down in a spacious place where we can be the people we were created to be. We are meant to be a free and favored sons and daughters of the King with big dreams in the Kingdom. With God's hand in ours, he reverses our destiny from one of our choosing to one of his choosing, for life on this side of the great divide as well as for eternity. It is a kind of life no eye has seen, no ear has heard, and no mind has conceived. He loves us and wants to show us. Let him.

SOMETHING TO PONDER

Take time to consider your destiny at this moment in your life. God is your destiny if you choose to let him take control.

God can provide a reversal for you. It will be a new thing. Do you perceive it? Remember Isaiah 43:18-19, "Forget the former things; do not dwell on the past. See, I am doing a new thing! Now it springs up; do you not perceive it? I am making a way in the wilderness and streams in the wasteland."

Daily Living in Truth, Trust, and Freedom

The Walk with God

What is worship? Worship is praising God, admiring and thanking God, reverencing God, and walking with God. It is remembering who God is, what he is like, what he has done, and how he has been faithful.

Lately God has been changing my way of thinking about worship, and also about life and what he desires me to do in it. God is teaching me to praise him and thank him when I am working. In addition, when I am walking, praying, or studying Scripture, I can really think about who he is and what he is like. The Spirit of God brings to mind how he has been faithful, and he reminds me to give thanks for what is going on in my life today and in the lives of my family and friends and community.

I am coming to realize that worship is a way of living. God tells us to love him with all of our heart, soul, mind, and strength, and there is only one way to do this. It is to focus our hearts and minds on him and keep in relationship with him. If we focus on God in our daily lives, he becomes more and more real to us. Then we start talking to him first about things, and letting him guide us on the spiritual pathway. We were made for this kind of worship. When we find God, we know what we were made to do.

Keeping On

> Therefore we do not lose heart. Though outwardly we are wasting away, yet inwardly we are being renewed day by day. For our light and momentary troubles are achieving for us an eternal glory that far outweighs them all. So we fix our eyes not on what is seen, but on what is unseen, since what is seen is temporary, but what is unseen is eternal (2 Cor. 4:16-18).

This passage in Paul's Second Corinthians describes God's rich mercy amid our momentary worries and the hope we have for renewal and glory when things are tough. These words offer us great anticipation: we are not to lose heart; we are being renewed daily; our afflictions are light and fleeting; our glory is eternal; and, we can perceive the things that are usually not perceived. The unseen in heaven and the seen on earth are God's plan to make us into the creatures we were created to be, creatures surrendered to him by the sacrificial death of Christ on the cross for our sins. Because we cannot carry the burdens of this world, the Son of God shoulders them for us and teaches us that the troubles he allows are small and short-lived compared to the riches the Father has planned for us in his house (John 14:2).

Courage to keep on keeping on is gift from God. He sustains us to not lose heart by giving us extra hope in our hearts when we can't see his design for us. He shares in our struggles to make it and helps us wait on and hope for the unseen. He supplies courage so we can fix our eyes on him, and with courage comes a new start, a beginning closer to the goal. A new faith shapes our vision giving us a sharper glimpse of eternity. God renews us daily and transforms us into a purer image reflecting more of the divine splendor. That image is purified, and the act of becoming like him achieves for us an amazing glory in eternity like nothing we can imagine. Our hope in the unseen becomes the focus by which we grow and are purified for the Kingdom. Glory be to God!

God is holy and awesome and has done an amazing work through his Son. His work allows us to participate in his glory on earth, achieving for us an eternal glory in heaven.

Becoming

God is good. He covers us when we are guilty. He hides us when we are fearful of the Enemy. He provides for us always, and is our shelter, refuge, and rock. He pursues us to bring us close, safe, and secure. We cannot go outside of God's care. He knows our very frame, our thoughts, and our words before we utter them.

What keeps us from crying out to this good, faithful, and accessible God? Where should we go but to him? What are we seeking that we don't go to him? In my personal case, I know I am sometimes afraid to ask God again about something I have asked him before but that I still can't get right. Here is what I often forget: God remembers our sins no more. He is merciful and faithful to forgive us when we come to him I prayer. We may be counting the times we have asked him about something, but he isn't. When we come, he opens his heart to us. Why don't we open ours to him? What God wants is for us to trust him with the difficult things in our lives. He wants us to know that instead of hiding the hard stuff we can bring it to light so he can take us through whatever peaks or valleys the journey requires to set us free. If there is something we are seeking more than we are seeking God, we are going to be sorely disappointed. It will not be

God doing the disappointing, but things other than God will. He says to seek him, know him, and love him, and that is what he means.

God wired us to be connected to our Creator. When we pour our love into other things or beings above the one supreme God, we are missing out on the one thing that brings us joy, peace, and freedom. Nothing and no one is as faithful as God. Nothing and no one offers love that is more lasting. Sometimes I get things turned upside down, but God constantly reminds me with his Word placed on my heart. I can't get too far without him or too much into my own thing without his Word coming to mind. When the Bible speaks to my heart, it rearranges and disentangles my muddled thoughts.

God has a plan for our lives that includes abundant living and freedom. To know the Master is to know abundance and freedom in serving the one living Christ. Do we want purpose, meaning, and fruitfulness in our lives? His love brings these things with it so much more than we imagine. It uncovers more desire in us than we dreamed was inside us. When we receive the love God has for us, his grace and truth become real and powerful in our lives. Faith is born and grows, and the Word of God becomes light to us. We love him and want to know him more. He becomes our life.

WE PRAISE HIM

> You, God, are my God, earnestly I seek you; I thirst for you, my whole being longs for you, in a dry and parched land where there is no water. I have seen you in the sanctuary and beheld your power and your glory. Because your love is better than life, my lips will glorify you. I will praise you as long as I live, and in your name I will lift up my hands. I will be fully satisfied as with the richest of foods; with singing lips my mouth will praise you (Ps. 63:1-5).

Life does not satisfy or quench our desires for more, but God does. His love is better than life and it is what fills us up to satisfaction. The psalmist David says it well when he sings praises to God as the only One who is praiseworthy. He is filled with praise for God who gives the richest of foods in a dry and weary land where there is no water. God quenches the thirst of David's soul.

What a great God we have, always drawing us in. When we seek him earnestly, when we come to listen and to be filled, he gives us spiritual nourishment. When we receive him, we are humbled and awed that we can have a personal relationship with our great God who is holy and separated from sin but who nevertheless is fully accessible to us. All we can do at this point is to worship him. God placed in us a need to worship, and he placed in us a need for the divine. God desires our worship for himself and for us. We cannot *not* praise Him.

"I tell you," Jesus said, "if they keep quiet, the stones will cry out" (Luke 19:40). The mental picture of rocks crying out if we don't praise God puts us in mind of the time of God's coming. Imagine a day when all of creation shouts in worship of our Creator and King, the King of glory.

Father God, don't let our mental images or small ideas of you limit our praise. Help us to earnestly seek you to know you better and broaden our understanding of who we think you are. Help us to praise you with humble hearts and minds in a way that pleases you and you only. Thank you for allowing us to participate in your glory and holiness as we come to you with praise.

GOD ALONE IS PRAISEWORTHY

> You turned my wailing into dancing; you removed my
> sackcloth and clothed me with joy, that my heart may sing

your praises and not be silent. Lord my God, I will praise
you forever. (Ps. 30:11-12).

After meeting God and being drawn to him over and over,
which is the same thing as living in relationship with him, his love
and mercy become one's daily bread. He is our portion and our cup,
and he makes our lives secure (Ps. 16:5). I am reminded of how God
entices me into his presence with a Scripture I have read over and
over but then, reading it once again, it has brand new meaning. I
know he is going to show me something that will be heart-changing
and life-altering. Praying with gratitude even in the darkest of hours
becomes part of life because the Lord is there. He *is*, and that's all
that matters.

We are told that the stones will cry out if we don't praise the Lord
(Luke 19:40). All of planet Earth and God's creation shout his name:
Ascribe to the Lord, O MIGHTY ONES,
ascribe to the Lord glory and strength.
Ascribe to the Lord the glory due his name;
worship the Lord in the splendor of his holiness.
The voice of the Lord is over the waters;
the God of glory thunders,
the Lord thunders over the mighty waters.
The voice of the Lord is powerful;
the voice of the Lord is majestic.
The voice of the Lord breaks the cedars;
the Lord breaks in pieces the cedars of Lebanon.
He makes Lebanon skip like a calf,
Sirion like a young wild ox.
The voice of the Lord strikes
with flashes of lightning.
The voice of the Lord shakes the desert;

the Lord shakes the Desert of Kadesh.
The voice of the Lord twists the oaks
and strips the forests bare.
And in his temple all cry, "Glory!"
The Lord sits enthroned over the flood;
the Lord is enthroned as King forever.
The Lord gives strength to his people;
the Lord blesses his people with peace (Ps. 29).

In the thirtieth psalm David knows gratitude of the heart, mind, and soul in God's presence. He knows that while circumstances are changing, God is not changing and that he will always be there. "You turned my wailing into dancing; you removed my sackcloth and clothed me with joy, that my heart may sing to you and not be silent. O Lord my God, I will give you thanks forever" (30:11-12).

Will we be there to praise the Lord and not be silent? God loves us and wants us to have a heart, mind, and soul that love him. He wants to give us a heart that desires his presence, and a mind, soul, and strength that hangs on and perseveres in the race that is the end-all of races …so that we will sing and not be silent.

PRAYER OF THE HEART THAT WANTS TO KNOW HIM

Father God, I want to know you. Will you give me a heart that desires you above all else? I know my heart is not available in the ways you would want, but make me and mold me into a person who loves you with all my heart, soul, mind, and strength.

You are loving and kind and are the sovereign God of all creation. You are faithful and you never change. You are who you say you are. Thank you for your love, your mercy, and your truth. Change me. Help me to surrender. Your hope will not disappoint.

MORE THAN WE IMAGINED

> My ears had heard of you but now my eyes have seen you
> (Job 42:5).

What if God's unveiling was more than we ever hoped or imagined? God says in his Word that the unveiling occurred in the death and resurrection of Jesus Christ and now occurs in the indwelling of the Holy Spirit in the hearts of believers. We may approach the Father with confidence that our hope, Jesus Christ, is our anchor, firm and secure. God has allowed us to come into his presence with unveiled faces through his Son Jesus Christ. But some of us come before him with veils covering our hearts in places we don't want to see and definitely don't want him to enter. This saddens God and keeps us from the treasure he has waiting for us. We are like the small child in trouble who looks away from her mother hoping she cannot be seen.

If we believe God at his Word, then we can approach with confidence, knowing he already knows us, though our frames be as dust. Like Job, when we recognize God for who he is, we will not only have heard of him, but now we see him. When we face our deepest fear of being unworthy to be in God's presence (which we are, as only God is perfect and worthy), then we come empty-handed and receive his worthiness.

Unveiling our waywardness, hurts, and desires, and then letting them out in the light of God's cover, we become divine image-bearers. He has already carried all our sins to the cross, so we have no business still trying to carry them ourselves with heavy hearts and minds mirroring shadows of dark and light. Instead, we are to mirror to the world the Lord's glory: "And we, who with unveiled faces all reflect the Lord's glory, are being transformed into his likeness with ever-increasing glory, which comes from the Lord, who is the Spirit" (2 Cor. 3:18). Where the Spirit is, there is freedom.

The unveilings are manifold; the Almighty and Holy God is accessible to us, we come to him with confidence and unveiled faces, and he gives us freedom to come, worship, and obey him. By receiving our holy yet accessible Father God in Jesus Christ, who allows us beyond the veil and covers us with himself, we see with unveiled faces.

The Walk in Trust

> Trust in the Lord with all of your heart and lean not on your own understanding (Prov. 3:5).

I have linked understanding and trust my whole life. Perhaps it was the way I grew up, or maybe it is because I am a thinker by nature. In any event, God says the two don't necessarily go together. He says we must trust him and not lean on our own understanding. Early on in my childhood, I did not feel I could trust. This grew over into my adolescence early adulthood. I relied upon my thinking and understanding to move forward, even moving forward, I thought, in faith. God was always there leading and guiding me, but I did not always trust him. Thinking we understand everything can get us into trouble. We cannot understand God's ways or his thoughts. He gives us his Word and he gives us faith to help us understand his plans. With every step of faith we take, God increases our trust in him. We may not know where we are going, but we can trust he does, and furthermore that he will never leave or forsake us.

When we are young, we develop patterns of coping with things we do not understand. Sometimes the methods we use are not good, especially when we depend on our own strength or understanding to go the next step. We develop insight into the behavior of others in order to please them. We use our own intuition to maintain peace and easier relationships. God certainly gives us minds and intuitions, but what he wants us to depend on is our trust in him. I have developed intuition and strong adaptations to cope in my family of origin. But that hasn't always gotten me very far. God doesn't want me to lean on my own understanding but to trust him in all things. His strength has to overcome my weakness. I must yield so he can transform me into a woman not of understanding but of trust. Understanding is something that God does best; it is too difficult for me. "My heart is not proud, O Lord, my eyes are not haughty; I do not concern myself with great matters or things too wonderful for me" (Ps. 131:1).

LOVING AND OBEYING AND SWEET SURRENDER TO GOD

Loving and obeying requires letting go of our will and surrendering to God's will. We make active decisions every day to go to work or play hooky, to eat healthy foods or pile on the calories, to go to the grocery store, to visit a friend in the hospital, and the list goes on and on. Sometimes we make decisions by *not* actively making them. For example, when we don't go to the grocery store, we will have to eat out or go without, or eat with someone else.

Whether we have an affection for them or not, loving our neighbor or family member is a decision. God tells us that "we should love one another" (1 John 3:11). If we are to honor and love God, we must love others. The first key is to make the decision to do so. We are not told to love only those who love us, or love those we feel like loving. We are told to love one another. This means we are to love even our enemies: "But love your enemies, do good to them, and lend to them without expecting to get anything back. Then your reward will be great, and you will be sons of the Most High, because he is kind to the ungrateful and wicked" (Luke 6:35). If we are to love our enemies, we first have to make the decision to love them. We have to consciously determine that it is something we will do even when we don't feel like it—because God tells us that we must.

Loving and obeying requires forgiving. Forgiving someone who has wronged us is a difficult thing, but here again God tells us to do it. "Do not judge, and you will not be judged. Do not condemn, and you will not be condemned. Forgive, and you will be forgiven" (Luke 6:37). And, "When you stand praying, if you hold anything against anyone, forgive him, so that your Father in heaven may forgive you your sins" (Mark 11:25). How do we forgive? God forgave us and in his great mercy he forgives us daily without remembering how we have been wrong. Can we forgive the same way?

Most of us can decide to forgive, but not necessarily to forget. Forgetting seems to be God's territory. We are to obey him in the decision to forgive, but we do have the capacity to remember how God has forgiven us over and over again, as well as the capacity to remember how grateful we were when we forgave someone else. We can remind ourselves that we have forgiven the person a particular wrong every time the memory presents itself. We can ask God to make us grateful for this decision, and to remember it with gratitude. God can turn ruins into new things. Only he can do this, but we have to be willing to make the change. By forgiving others with his mercy, we are making this first step. We may have to forgive again, and indeed we will have to forgive again. We will have to forgive over and over. It is a daily thing.

Loving and obeying requires giving up our hopes and dreams and putting them in the hands of God. When we are willing to do that, God says he will put a song in our hearts. "He put a new song in my mouth, a hymn of praise to our God. Many will see and fear and put their trust in the Lord" (Ps. 40:3). God will give us the desires of our hearts if we will commit ourselves to him. He has great dreams for us and he wants us to have our hope not in our dreams but in his. The things of this world, including our own dreams, will disappoint, but God never will.

Loving and obeying requires more than giving up our hopes and dreams. It requires giving up disappointment. We don't want to be disappointed by life or people or situations, so why would we want to hold on to disappointment? When things do not turn out the way we expect, we feel angry or abandoned. We want things to turn around. We try fixing them, not remembering them. If we remember them, we become resentful and don't address the disappointment straight on. God wants us to trust him in *all things*, in hurt and disappointment too. Our trying to fix things or people is our way of controlling and not trusting. God wants us to allow him into our hurts to help us heal and move away from our disappointments. We are to forgive so the Lord can abide in us to help us through the pain and disappointment. That is the way to hope.

Giving up disappointments means giving our hearts and minds over to God and allowing him to replace our thoughts and desires with his own. We have to trust him with the "replacements." In order to trust him we must know him, love him, and obey him. When we decide to take the first step allowing him to take the disappointment from us, he will do the rest. Our willingness is an act of faith, and he can and will grow this tiny mustard seed of heart willingness into bigger acts of obedience.

Loving and obeying requires letting go of past hurt. As I have written, my mother has contempt toward me. This has been extremely hurtful through the years, not to mention exhausting when I must communicate with her about personal things. Because I have never been able to figure out why she is contemptuous, I agonize over what I have done to cause it. This, however, is a vicious cycle that cannot be overcome by me alone. When I have tried understanding why or tried fixing it with more attention or more pleasing behavior (on her terms), I get sucked into exchanges that are impossible to manage because of her unreasonable demands and expectations. I want to be free of the hurt and the disruption that it causes in my life. More importantly, I want peace and harmony for my mother and for our relationship. I lived far too long in self-preservation mode, and I finally determined that this life was not pleasing to God because I did not trust him in my relationship with her.

Only by praying and interceding for the one who is perpetrating the harm can we become vessels in this war. When Jesus introduced himself as the Son of God, he was spat upon, hit, despised, and ridiculed. He was without fault, without guile, and without sin, and yet he was slain on our behalf. He said we would have suffering and pain and that we would have to pray for our enemies. He prayed for his killers as he was dying on the cross. He said they did not know what they were doing. God wants to use us in a way that is more powerful, more compassionate, more glorifying to him than we can imagine. We must surrender our own attitudes when we are despairing, hurting, or suffering loss or relationship. He says he will not disappoint. The journey he has for us is desiring him above all else, turning our faces to him in hope, and letting our hearts be full of Christ instead of expecting it from other places.

By faith, I have hope. When I hurt, am disappointed, exhausted, and weary of the contempt, God wants me to cry out for his mercy and truth. He will do the rest. He may take away my mother's contempt, or he may not. He may give me more love and blessing as I turn from her contempt to his unfailing love. We keep turning to him who never turns away, who never abandons, and who never shows contempt for his children. His love is now and everlasting. As He loves, I am able to love. He can teach me to pray as he would for another. When I don't know how to pray, he does it on my behalf. As long as I am willing, he is able. This is *hope*.

Lord, help me to be willing today to be your vessel, one of love, mercy, truth, and hope. Make me willing to surrender this hurt to you. Lord, only you are able to handle this situation, for it is beyond my ability or understanding. Help me to lean wholly on you.

LEANING ON GOD'S UNDERSTANDING, NOT OUR OWN

God understands and is sovereign over all. We question and we wonder what about this, or what about that, in order to understand something. As human beings we like to understand as much as we can, and to fix things if they do not suit us. And if we cannot understand, we want to do something to make things different. But God did not call us to make a way for ourselves. He says he will make a way for us, lead us on unfamiliar paths, and give us enough light and guidance to take each step.

LIVING THROUGH THE CIRCUMSTANCES

As God's children, we do not have to live under the circumstances. Rather, we can live through the circumstances in victory. God can lead us and guide us, and at the same time he can keep us at peace during difficult circumstances. In order to live through some things, we have to give up an illusion of control. Because we do not have real control over trying situations, some of us act in more domineering ways to live above circumstances instead of living under them. Yet the Bible says that God wants us to trust him completely in all things: "In God I trust; I will not be afraid. What can man do to me?" (Ps. 56:11). "Trust in him at all times, O people; pour out your hearts to him, for God is our refuge" (Ps. 62:8). "May the God of hope fill you with all joy and peace as you trust in him, so that you may overflow with hope by the power of the Holy Spirit" (Rom. 15:13). Little by little we can give over our controlling nature to the Lord as we take steps to trust and believe him.

As we walk each day, we must live in the present, not the past or the future. We can only live in this day that the Lord has made. He asks us to rejoice and be glad in it (Ps. 118:24), because he made it for us to use for his glory. Whatever is in front of us, God can use it for his glory so long as we choose to let him be sovereign over our affairs. We will have hope if we allow him full authority in our lives. Our own expectations do not measure up to what God has planned for us. He knows what has come before, what is coming after, and all in between. He is using the whole kit and caboodle for his will and work, and none of it will be wasted. He wants us to trust him with all outcomes.

God also tells us to thank him for all things and to keep praising him, that is, to pray at all times with all faith. He does not want us to analyze things in order to deal with them—we are to leave that to him. His Word in the book of Isaiah says, "As the heavens are higher than the earth, so are my ways higher than your ways and my thoughts than your thoughts" (55:9). The psalmist also admits that the things of God are greater than his understanding, and no wonder. God is in control, and we need no other.

LIVING ANOTHER'S PAIN OR STRUGGLE— STANDING IN HOPE AND SURRENDER

God requires that we have compassion and care for each other. He also wants us to intercede for one another. When someone is in pain or going through a difficult time, our first response is to help that person, to fix the situation and make it better. We may be able to offer help and assistance in many different ways, but what if there is nothing we can do to alleviate the suffering? In that case we can stand with that person and pray for them. God wants us to be mediators, to pray on behalf of others, and to care for them. We are to stand with each other during the good times and bad, caring for and interceding for one another.

Sometimes we have certain ways that are deeply engrained in our relationships, especially with family members or a spouse. How we support them is not always in accord with how God would have us love them or support them. His ways are not our ways and his thoughts are not our thoughts. God wants us to depend on him in how we go through our own pain and how we go through it with others. We are to trust him with the person who is struggling and give to them the care and encouragement that is led by God. Sometimes the Lord administers his love through us, and sometimes through others, but in the final analysis he wants to bring us all to him for his care and love.

LIVING WITH HOPE

To live in hope of God's design for life we have to be surrendered to the Redeemer. He wants all parts of our lives, not just the parts we want to relinquish. I know he is patient and he is peeling away the layers in my life. I am amazed at how lovingly he reveals the places

I haven't allowed for him to go in my life. The silly part is that he already knows about them and what made me the way I am. I just haven't let him into those places yet—I haven't given him control of those areas. I also know that God is so amazingly on time. If it is time for me to let go of a certain thing in my life, the Lord will make that happen in various ways—maybe through closing doors in my face or through my falling flat on my face. I would rather he gradually reveal things for me to get the message rather than shut something down without notice. Wouldn't we all?

God is God and he *is*. Isn't it funny that we question God? Not one of us is in a position to question the God of the universe, and yet he allows us to question, doubt, express anger and frustration, and even wrestle with him. But it is strange logically that we would do so. That is part of God's design, too. God knows we need to decide on our own, through our own free will, whether or not to live for him. After all, he made us and knows our needs and desires before we do.

The Lord wants us all to live in hope in a personal relationship with him. When we are in relationship with the One who knows us like no other, and when we allow him to lead us daily, we will walk in places we have not been before and be used for his kingdom in ways we would never have dreamed. This relationship puts us in heavenly communion with the God of the universe.

Truth is found in God Only

Seeking Truth

God places in us a desire for truth, and it this desire for truth that gives us a conscience. The conscience may be hidden deeply under many layers of living, so to speak, but it is there because we know the difference between right and wrong. In addition to knowing right and wrong, we know there is absoluteness in the authority and deity of God. He is Truth and there is no other.

In order to know truth, we must seek after God while he is near. There is no other way to know the God of absolute Truth except by seeking, by calling to him and seeking after his heart.

Abiding in His Presence

In order to abide in Christ's presence, I must keep my thoughts on what is honorable, right, true, lovely, and good. He is always there, yet still I must seek him to remain in his presence. I must have a humble heart, an obedient spirit, and an alert mind. God speaks and reveals himself to those desiring to hear him and know him.

If I surrender my heart, mind, and soul to the Lord, I will enjoy his peace. He resides in us when we ask him into our lives, and we will only enjoy real freedom as we learn to honor and respect his presence. As he lives in us and we experience him, we want more and more of the divine company. If we allow him more of us and we ask to love him more and to know him better, God will give us the full knowledge of and the complete freedom in him. The ultimate fulfillment of these desires will be in heaven and everlasting union with God. But here and now God wants us to taste and see that he is good and that his love endures forever on this side of eternity. Abiding in the presence of God is a great privilege for us on earth. Knowing him like this is a mystery and the hope for which we long.

LIVING IN TRUTH

When we allow God to be who he is in us, we are becoming who he desires us to be. God wants us to be fully alive, living in love instead of fear. He loves all his children equally and wants us to see others as he sees them.

To live in this truth we must let go of our lives as we see them and risk living the life he has planned for us. We are to be bold in God's authority, for he gave us his authority to use in his name for his glory. When we have God's truth and authority, and when we use it according to his plans and purposes, Jesus says we will do greater works than even he did in his earthly ministry.

What is truth? God is truth. Scripture is truth. We find truth when we seek the Lord in all earnestness. He gives discernment to all who ask, and wisdom to all who seek. The Word of God gives us direction as we seek to live in truth.

We are to live in the world but not of the world. Jesus said, "I have given them your word and the world has hated them, for they are not of the world any more than I am of the world" (John 17:14). We must be armed with the power of the blood of Jesus in the Holy Spirit, with God's truth as our armor.

Three Things Needed for Running the Race

When my daughter and I participate in 10K races, we want to be physically prepared—even if we are just going to be walking the race instead of running. The weather and the environment are factors during parts of the year, and another factor is the number of people participating. The last race we took part in had eighty thousand-plus. As I prepare, it makes me think about all the ways we must be ready for life with its twists and turns. Will my body be ready to withstand the heat and the terrain of the race? What do I take with me to drink, and how do I make myself ready for the crowd and the excitement of the race? These are just a few of the questions that apply also as we approach daily living. How do we prepare for living to withstand the hard circumstances? What do we take with us each day to make good decisions, to have better communications, and to build right relationships? God says he has given us all we need for daily living if we believe in him and trust him. He has also given us instructions in his Book about knowing, believing, and trusting the Author of the Book.

If we believe God, we want to spend time in his presence and in his Word. We want to know him, and as we spend time in prayer and in Scripture, God hides his Word in our hearts. Spending time in the presence of God is preparing our hearts for life's race, and it is the number one thing on the list of what we need to do to become strong disciples of Christ. It is our choice to do this, and when we do God takes our little steps and makes them big ones. He changes our hearts to be fit for the race of life and all that it brings.

Depending on God in the valleys and on the mountains, the successes and the failures become the vehicle God uses to help us endure the race. The number two thing on the list of what we need to do to become strong disciples of Christ is the experience of depending on God and leaning on him like no other. Again, it is a choice we make to depend on him, gratitude for the day, for the good and the bad, and prayerful reliance to give us the strength for whatever comes. The discipline practices being dependent, grateful, and prayerfully focused on the provider and not the provision. The discipline of dependence, surrender, and prayerful focus on the One who is the author and finisher or perfecter of our faith is the best preparation for life's race, and it is the number three thing on the list of what we need to do to become strong disciples of Christ. It is like a packing list for the journey of life—God's place in our hearts, our dependence on him, and then the daily practice of the other two. Are we ready for life's race? If so, then "Let us fix our eyes on Jesus, the author and perfecter of our faith, who for the joy set before him endured the cross, scorning its shame, and sat down at the right hand of the throne of God" (Heb. 12:2).

READY, SET, GO

Do we wake up ready to go in the morning? Most of the time, I don't. Sometimes I am not looking forward to the things of the day. And then sometimes I just want more time to get ready. I'm a planner and organizer by nature, and this can become a crutch to delay my getting things done. I just like order so much. God says he has given us what we need in order to run the race of life. He tells us in Hebrews 12:1-2 that we are to throw off what hinders us and to focus on Christ Jesus: "Therefore, since we are surrounded by such a great cloud of witnesses, let us throw off everything that hinders and the sin that so easily entangles, and let us run with perseverance the race marked out for us. Let us fix our eyes on Jesus, the author and perfecter of our faith, who for the joy set before him endured the cross, scorning its shame, and sat down at the right hand of the throne of God." My need for order and control is a hindrance to running my race and I must throw off the things that hinder me.

God has given us what we need to run the race and to serve him in this world. The apostle Paul tells us in 2 Timothy 1:6-7 that we are to use the gifts God has given us to reach others. He writes, "For this reason I remind you to fan into flame the gift of God, which is in you through the laying on of my hands. For God did not give us a spirit of timidity, but a spirit of power, of love and of self-discipline." My need for order and control is not the self-discipline or sound mind of which Paul speaks. Instead, it is the spirit of timidity. Have I really received a spirit of love, power, and a sound mind? Have you? When we learn from Scripture such as Hebrews 12:1-2 and 2 Timothy 1:6-7 how to run the race of life, do we take God at his Word?

The three things we have been given to run with perseverance the race marked out for us are a spirit of power, love, and self-discipline (a sound mind). God loves us freely and has given us the capacity to *love* freely also. With this the Lord gives us the ability to forgive and to love unconditionally. We have the capacity to choose to love and to forgive through Christ Jesus. With the truth and mercy of Jesus within us by his Spirit we can love as he loved us. Through the death and resurrection Christ we have the *power* of God's outstretched arm, and within us the Holy Spirit. It is resurrection-from-the-dead power with truth and mercy intertwined, and it speaks the truth in love by sharing it boldly and freely. God gives us a *sound mind*, one that knows divine revealed truth through his Word and one that knows his Word resides in our hearts. The sound mind through the Holy Spirit within us helps us remember God's truth in his Word and what he has done in our world. With sound minds, we know him, believe him, and serve him.

Prayer: Father God, thank you for your gifts of love, power, and a sound mind. Help me to receive them from you this day. Help me to fan into flames these gifts so I can be a benefit to your Kingdom. Give me a grateful heart and make me ready to serve you today. Thank you for loving me.

CLEANING OUT CLUTTER

Cleaning out clutter is therapeutic to me. The order that comes from throwing things out and getting things neatened up and into their own places gives me a kick. It is a mystery why I let things build up when I know the thrill of bringing order from chaos. Cleaning out the basement is like dealing with one's inner self. There are certain things most of us don't want to deal with or think about that frighten us or make us feel uncomfortable. We would rather put off dealing with them. On the other hand, when we do face unpleasant things head on, they usually turn out being not as bad as we think they will be. For me, the feeling of satisfaction I get when I face uncertainty or handle a situation I have been dreading is a great sense of accomplishment, not unlike getting rid of clutter.

When the mind is full of things that get in the way of one's progress, whether in work or in life, it is like clutter. Hebrews 12:1 tells Christians to "throw off everything that hinders and the sin that so easily entangles, and let us run with perseverance the race marked out for us." God wants us to be free of all that takes up space in our lives and keeps us from him and the plans he has for us. According to the prophet Jeremiah, these plans are "to prosper you and not to harm you, plans to give you hope and a future" (Jer. 29:11). When I am fearful or holding onto anxious thoughts, I am not free to know and see what God has for me. My heart and mind are not available for truth and freedom and all the things that enable me. At the same time, my mind and heart are filled with something, and so I have to choose which things I am going to allow in my conscious thoughts.

Cleaning out clutter of the mind and the heart can be as therapeutic as cleaning out the basement or the garage. Letting go of past hurts and placing them in God's hands in order for him to heal and restore us to wholeness is a huge step. Also, to forgive someone of a wrong creates a whole new place in our hearts for God's love and truth. When we relinquish something harmful, God can replace it with newness and hope. I want to clean out the clutter in my heart as well as the clutter of my home. If I free my mind for God's truth and put into practice the words of Scripture, the Father will help me recall the Word when I need it because the Bible says he has written his Word on our hearts. Why would I create such havoc in my mind and heart with clutter when heavenly treasure already resides in me?

PAIN AND WHERE WE PUT IT

The veterinary hospital recently kept our golden retriever overnight. She's such a happy and sweet dog; everyone who meets her loves her. On her last visit she had a tumor removed from her mouth, and because of this the veterinarian was reticent about examining her mouth, which is a normal reluctance after having surgery. It made me think about our pain, physical and emotional, and how we deal with it. Our golden retriever trusts us and the doctors to treat her well because she has no options. The veterinarian said she pouted a little about the examination, her way of saying she did not like it. But that was the extent of what she could do to object. How do we say we don't like pain?

One way some of us express that we don't like emotional pain is not to express anything. If we refuse to talk about it, maybe it won't be there. Or if it is there, maybe it will go away. We also avoid emotional pain by working around it. In working around a painful thing, we create other chasms that can bring on more pain. This becomes a vicious cycle, which in some cases develops into a generational curse because the emotional pain is not faced. As for physical pain, we also handle it by avoidance and working around it. But we also handle the pain by medicating it. Each method has its problems. For instance, if one hurts the knee and then tries compensating by not moving the knee a certain way, another part of the leg gets the brunt of the workload and this might cause another injury. For pain of a more emotional nature, what if each time we experience emotional hurt we transferred the hurt to eating or drinking? Overeating and drinking too much are obvious health risks.

Our golden retriever has to trust us with her health and well-being, even if she does not like it. She cannot avoid the pain of a tumor removal because the veterinarian is going to take it out. What do we do with pain when we know we have to trust God for our physical and emotional well-being? We must bring it to God, who wants either to carry the burden of the pain for us or take it out. Where do we put our pain when we know we have to trust? We put it at the feet of Jesus, who knows all about pain. Putting it there is the place of total surrender, where all is left to be conquered, healed, restored, and forgiven. When he takes the pain from us, he fills the hole where the pain used to be. Who will we trust with our pain, and where will we put it?

FLAILING OR FLOURISHING

When a living creature has the things it needs to thrive, it flourishes. Have you ever seen a plant so green and healthy it made you examine its soil and sunlight so you could replicate the conditions? Or have you observed a child in a setting making her laugh and create and play with joy and thought you were witnessing her "in her element." On my morning walks I am sometimes stunned by the magnificence of three amazingly green and beautiful ferns that have been shielded from the bright summer sun in a grove of trees. Yet the huge sprawling ferns are flourishing in the shade of the trees and the dampness of a nearby creek. I wonder what I need in my work environment to flourish like that.

I start out the school year making sure I create a healthy and stable home environment for my children to thrive in their school and home life. Part of my job is to create a safe haven for them and my husband when he returns home after a long day. Am I doing the same for myself? It has made me think of a bigger question: What am I doing to create an environment where we can all flourish in our spiritual lives? God creates an environment for us to thrive, to live in freedom for his purposes. Just as the green and abundant ferns find life in the grove, we can find life in relationship to God through Christ. We will flourish if we spend time with him, learn his ways from his Word, and believe and obey him with our decisions and our direction. If our focus becomes something else, we begin faltering and flailing in our daily lives.

The Lord says that no matter where we are, "Never will I leave you; never will I forsake you" (Heb. 13:5). Flourishing is a matter of believing and following him, but, on the other hand, following our own paths leads to threshing around aimlessly. The child "in her element" finds true joy, laughter, and creativity. The psalmist says: "But I am like an olive tree flourishing in the house of God; I trust in God's unfailing love for ever and ever. For what you have done I will always praise you in the presence of your faithful people. And I will hope in your name, for your name is good" (Ps. 52:8-9).

Let us trust in God's unfailing love and praise him for his goodness to us.

WEATHERING

Summertime is not my favorite season for walking. The heat is quite a test, but God uses it to temper me and show me he is in control. I am just to walk and continue walking. Life and faith are like that, too. If we awaken for another day, we have to keep on keeping on. If we are believers, we put one foot in front of the other and continue on the journey he has for us, even if that journey is not to our satisfaction at the moment. We might not like the valleys or the mountain climbing or the storms, but that is where God has us at this point, and so we carry on.

Some mornings I feel called to wait on God. I surrender all that is in me after a couple of weeks of wrestling with him, and I wait and continue waiting until he shows me his hand. He is in control of my life and I want to keep it that way. Even when the journey is difficult, the days long, and I don't think that he hears me, I want to be surrendered to his way and his walk for me. So I keep walking until he gives me the assurance he is there walking with me and that I will be ready when he calls.

God is always with us. Faith is believing he hears our cries even when we don't think he hears. And faith is surrendering even when we don't feel like it. We will weather the storms because God will weather them with us. He gives us the cool breeze when we need the respite from the hot sun, and he allows the sun to beat on our backs when he is shaping us for what he has next. He has created us for his workmanship, for we are "an instrument for noble purposes, made holy, useful to the Master and prepared to do any good work" (2 Tim. 2:21). The Master molds us to allow the best in our lives, and our best will be for noble use.

Prayer: Father God, I thank you for your sovereignty and your grace, which allow me to cry out and wrestle with you, and I thank you for your faithfulness at all times. Keep me on your journey and help me surrender to you so you can use me for your noble purposes. Thank you for being with me always.

KimberlyGibsonJohnson

WEEDING THE GARDEN OF THE HEART

The springtime exhilarates me and gives me energy to do things
I don't normally do, like weeding the lawn. One afternoon after
cleaning out closets, I took some time in the sunshine to weed our
lawn. The grass was long, the weeds were overgrown, and in many
spots it was difficult to determine the grass from the weeds. In other
words, I had taken on a really big job.

A few years ago, my husband and I bought some huge rocks
to place in our yard as reminders of what God had done for us.
We placed the larger than one ton boulders in a strategic place in
our front yard, and we named them *Truth, Trust,* and *Freedom* for
a miraculous journey God guided our family through a few years
before. Just as the Israelites set up memorial stones at Gilgal after
crossing the Jordan to remind themselves of what God had done
for them, we wanted to remember and be grateful and to tell our
children how faithful and good God had been to us. Now weeds
had taken over the place where our memorial stones reside, and
Truth, Trust, and Freedom were being crowded out by sprawling
and vigorous plant growth. As I pulled up the resilient growth, it
came to me that while God's truth from his written Word resides in
my heart, other things continue growing there as well. I need to let
God cut the weeds out of my heart.

How does the overgrowth happen? It occurs when I let deceptive
thoughts and lies dwell there. The thought occurs and instead of taking
it captive to the transforming power of Christ, I let it remain. It grows
larger and spreads tenaciously. Some of the weeds are just on the top of
the soil, yet others have deep roots. The human heart has both deep-
rooted sin and shallow, new deceptive thinking patterns.

What does my heart look like to God when it is overgrown with
things that should not be there? Amidst the weeds other good things

are growing, but these things are not as strong or as widespread as they could be without all the rubbish, the weeds. I want to see the rocks in my front yard as reminders of the truth God has given us, the trust he has grown in our hearts, and the freedom he has given us throughout our journey with him. When the weeds have overtaken the location of the memorial stones, it is difficult to see them or even know they are there. And that is the way it is with believers.

Sometimes we Christians have so many others things growing in our hearts that others cannot see God's truth in our lives, or even see our trust in him in our attitudes or words. They can also miss seeing our freedom in Christ because we are so bound up by the thicket dwelling there. I pulled and cut and literally yanked the weeds from around our memorial stones, Truth, Trust, and Freedom. As I performed the front yard surgery, I asked God to make me mindful of his precious gifts of truth, trust, and freedom, and to be grateful to him always. At the same time I asked him to prune whatever is keeping these gifts from growing and flourishing in my heart and destroying the view of them to others who may need to see God's work in my life.

We need to see God's transforming work in our lives, the power of his truth, the grace of the trust he grows in us, and the freedom he gives us to live as his loving and obeying children. As we know and love the Lord, he grows us up to be like him for all the world to see.

WORDS HIDDEN IN MY HEART FROM GOD HIMSELF

God prayed through me in forgiveness of another who has harmed me. I have prayed the prayer of forgiveness for her many times, and I felt I had received the miracle of forgiveness. This was different; I was not in control. The Holy Spirit prayed the prayer through me. The words came out of my mouth aloud in the silence of my long country drive home. "Lord, forgive her; she does not know what she is doing," I prayed from my heart.

I was awed and humbled at the same time to be the vessel by which God prayed through me for her. It seemed as though I saw her differently, like I was the one in need of God's forgiveness. He was freeing me of my longing and my waiting and my need for peace with her. God can take the most undesirable parts of us and make them into something beautiful. In this case, it was the terrible ache inside of me to make things right. Only God can create new out of old, and right out of wrong. He did it in his own time, but it was also in perfect timing for me.

Before God prayed through me for this woman, I saw her as a disturbed person. "She was a disabled and damaged child," I said aloud to myself. "I am sorry that she is limited in this way; I hate that she has to suffer like this." At the same I knew that because of her limitations I was not in control of her suffering or her reaction to me. I could not make it right for either of us.

But God is sovereign. I think he ordered my thoughts on these occasions. He prepared my heart for his intervention. That is what God does—he prepares us, he goes before us, with us, and after us. When the words of forgiveness came out of my mouth, I knew they were God's, and I knew that God was acting on my behalf (and hers, too). It is a miracle, a gift from his heart to mine.

Camouflage vs. Coloratura

> Arise, shine, for your light has come, and the glory of the Lord rises upon you. See, darkness covers the earth and thick darkness is over the peoples, but the Lord rises upon you and his glory appears over you. Nations will come to your light, and kings to the brightness of your dawn (Isa. 60:1-3).

God makes himself known through his people. It is this mystery that confounds and exhilarates us, for God allows us to participate in the awesome and humbling mission of his work for his kingdom.

I noticed a new flowering plant on a neighborhood lawn. It was lilac in color with a center of toasty gold, lovely yet not brilliant to the eye. I was struck by its beauty, and at the same time I was puzzled by the thought that came to mind. My thought was that God kept my attention with all the brightly colored azaleas in bloom, even in the midst of my struggling to stay in his presence. Yet my attention was captured when I saw this beautiful flower that was less dazzling than the others. .

God's glory shines through his people, just as it does through the handiwork in creation. He does not desire for us to conceal his light in us. If we camouflage the work God has done in our lives by hiding who we are or what he has given us, we miss out on what he intends. He shows us his brilliance and his majesty, and he draws us by making himself known to us. He allows us to participate in his glory by using the gifts and talents he has given us to show the world who he is. He does not need us to exercise these gifts, and he does not command us to do so. But he allows us to be included in his kingdom plans.

The coloratura soprano is brilliant in ornamental embellishment of vocal music. When her vocal ability shines, it brings great pleasure to her audience. God does the same with his people in that he allows his gifts to shine in Christians so we can all see him in his glory and experience his presence. It is certainly true that God can use both camouflage and coloratura—or any other means—for his glory, but he desires that we be willing participants in his plan for the church and the world. Let his light shine for all the world to see. Let's be coloratura instead of camouflaged.

Desiring God

I cannot hold onto one thing and desire another. That would be like running the race and staying idle at the same time. I must lose what I cannot have in order to gain what I cannot obtain for myself. If I hold onto what is good, I may lose what is best. In my selfish desires, I may forgo God's best plan for me. In order to be healed or made whole, God may take some parts of me away to which I am attached. I may have to let go of a dream for myself in order to have God's dream. Trusting him is like saying that I will put my full weight on him as I jump into unknown territory and feel the free fall. He has me in his arms and will not let me plummet to the depths.

Desiring God is wanting a wholeness that only Christ can give. I want to know him fully, as fully as he knows me. If I let go of the familiar, he will give me light on the unfamiliar path that he designs. It is a path of truth and grace and courage and treasure. These are the things I want, and I will have them only in Christ. The Lord grants these things by his name and his blood, and only for his glory and his kingdom.

Deliverance Again ...More Victories

Why does it take so much to get me to my knees when I know with my heart and mind the rewards, blessings, and generosity of our God? Stated simply, it takes so long because I depend on my own sufficiency, my own direction, and my own desires. I need to depend on God, and that requires surrender.

Over the last years God has often reminded me how he brought me out of bondage and into freedom. Familiar paths of deceit and despair are well worn in my memory, but even fresher are the paths of freedom God has given me. When I choose to be grateful and remember what he has done, I am able to go the new way, his way with his leading. Then I begin being delivered to his journey set aside specifically for me. This choice includes letting go of what is important to me and taking hold of him. He is the answer to all the questions. I am to ask the questions, and then I am to listen. This sounds so simple and in fact it is very easy when I determine it is a choice I have to make daily in each thing that comes along.

My daughter's applications are due soon, and I want her to have the very best of everything. I know that is what God wants, too, even more than me. He wants her to have him more. How does she do that? She has to choose the Lord and let him take her where he wants her to go. I have to provide encouragement and care while she is in the throes of the application process. I must put aside my wishes and let God shape my desires for her as he molds her into the woman she is designed to be. As she sees me allow God to lead the way, she may also be more willing to let him lead the way in her life.

I told my daughter that we had encountered this same type of journey of faith before as a family, and God had provided *way* more than we ever expected. He is God and he knows what fulfills us more than we can know ourselves—because he made us. He has already provided more than can ever be expressed for us in Christ Jesus. He has already shown us his love and power in hundreds of ways. He wants my daughter to grow more in her faith through this next phase of her life. He is leading her to a new, spacious place he has already chosen for her, and he wants her to follow him to it. How does she do that? She must prepare her steps to include being open to divine guidance daily, to follow the things God puts in her path, and to relinquish her desires to his dreams for her.

The Father will lead her to the ultimate dream, and the ultimate dream is the one he planned for her before she was born. If she is open to him and chooses this path willingly, he will provide his presence, and heaven's plan will unfold. She will know God and his dream for her. It is all about her calling out and asking, seeking God's wisdom to know, and then following him to it. In fellowship with the Creator, she is a child of the King, one who is loved and given all she needs to be complete and fulfilled by the one and only true God.

God the Father, Son, and Holy Spirit is the One and Only. He must have the glory, and all things were made for his glory, including us. Whenever one of us tries bringing honor to himself or herself, or when we give another honor instead of God, we are allowing some of God's glory to be taken away. He is a jealous God, and he will not tolerate this. In our earnest prayers for our children, we need to ask that God's glory be shown in their lives, in our lives, and that nothing else and no one else will ever shine through them and us except the One and Only.

Bringing honor to God makes things a lot easier than trying to claim it for ourselves. After all, he *is* God and he will be glorified. What is required is for us to get out of the way and let him live in us and through us. I do not have control over what my children choose to do with their lives. But I have the option of helping them by encouraging them and by supporting them. More importantly, I can believe God and his promises concerning my children—who are really his children. God is sovereign and wants them where they will bring glory to him and be effective for the Kingdom; He also wants the same thing for me. With the Lord the pieces of the puzzle always fit and they always work to bring good. We may not understand God's plan, and we may not even want it, but it is God's plan. He never changes, and he will never leave us. We are delivered into his strong and loving arms. He is who we want; he continues to grow us up to know him. *Victory again, always, and already.*

Afterword: Come as a Child to the Father of all Hope

It is not intellect or sophistication that help us receive what the Father has to offer. It is childlike trust, receiving him and his love—his salvation ...and continuing to receive what he has to offer—rest, presence, peace, and joy.

When we come to Him

He gives us what He has to offer

More than we dreamed or imagined

Oh, how little we knew

He desires a spacious place for us

Rest in His presence and room to grow

All that He planned for us to be

Before the beginning and for His glory

If we believe as a child

He molds us from the inside out

To live safely and securely in His love

And in His care whatever the course

Life takes us up mountains and in valleys

But He is guiding, directing our steps whether

Steep or in mire, it seems, to keep us going

So that in time, we look back and see where He has carried us

And oh, the story He has written in our lives to be told

To our children and theirs for generations

Of how He planned for them a destiny beyond

All other because He is God and there is no other.

The world will know Him

Because He will show them

Through the lives of His children

Bold love, reversals, and redemption